Beaded Snowflake
Ornament Patterns

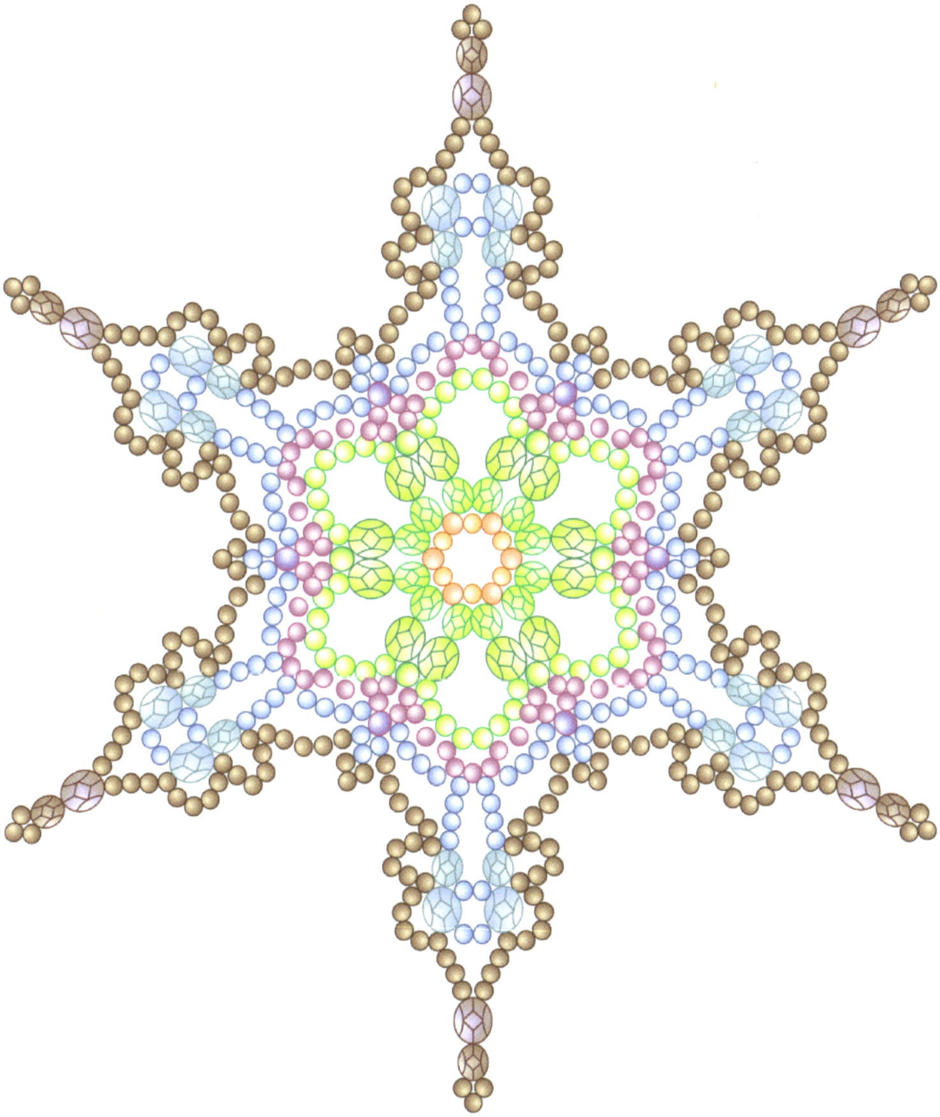

Sandra D. Halpenny

Beaded Snowflake Ornament Patterns
Copyright © 2022 Snowflake Designs and Illustrations, Sandra D. Halpenny
Canadian Intellectual Property Office
Certificate of Copyright Registration #1193247

Photographs Copyright © 2022, Sandra D. Halpenny, Donna Lawson, Rose Young
Patterns tested by: Julia Wentz

Published by: Sandra D. Halpenny
Beaded Snowflake Ornament Patterns
PRINT: ISBN 978-1-7782050-0-2
DIGITAL: ISBN 978-1-7782050-1-9

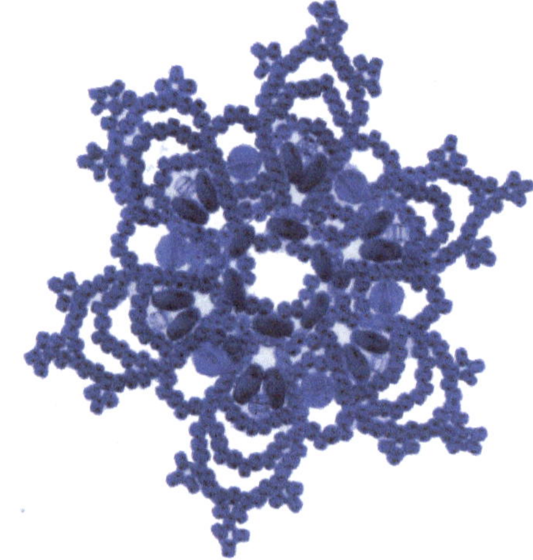

Glue Bottle Vectors by Vecteezy, https://www.vecteezy.com/free-vector/glue-bottle
Cover background photo is by: Ehsan ahmadnejad, https://unsplash.com/@ehsan_

Every effort has been made to ensure that all the information in this book is accurate. However, due to differing conditions, tools and individual skills, the publisher cannot be responsible for any injuries, losses or other damages that may result from the use of the information in this book.

The finished items made from this book can be made for personal use and for an individual's own pin money. You have my permission to make and sell at arts and craft shows, etc. No MASS production allowed. You may NOT teach classes from this book without written permission from the author.

Visit my web store for more patterns
http://www.SandraDHalpenny.com

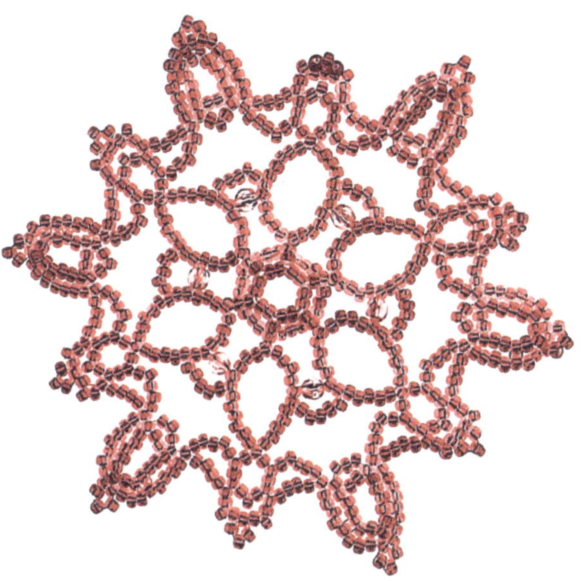

Dedication
This book is dedicated to 3 ladies that helped make this the most special snowflake pattern book.
None of these snowflake ornaments could have been designed and created without their help.

Thank you,
Julia Wentz
Donna Lawson
Rose Young

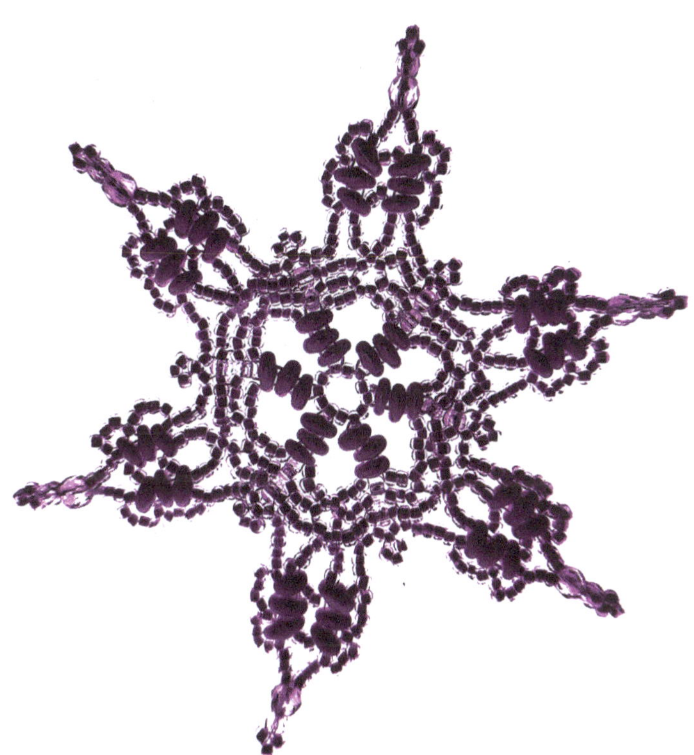

Table of Contents

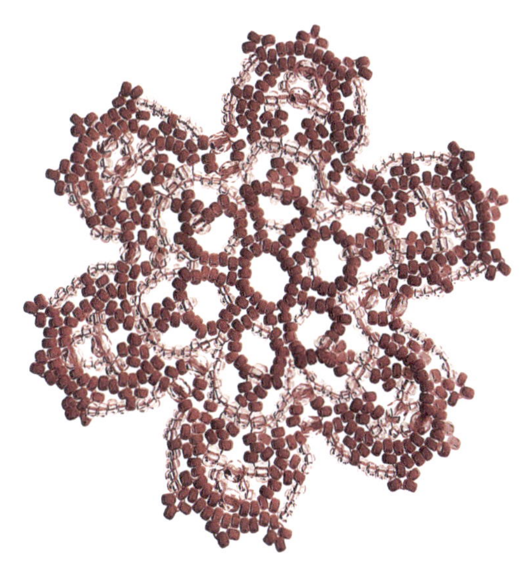

Getting Started

Gather Your Supplies

Beads

All my patterns are designed using Miyuki seed beads. I like to use these Japanese seed beads because they are uniform in size and the holes are large, even and wide enough to go through with thread several times.

Of course, you can use any kind of seed beads, but some of the patterns might need to be adjusted. Do a small section first to see how your seed beads will work.

For the snowflake ornaments in this book I have used mostly 11° seed beads. I have also used 8° and 15° seed beads and some 10° Triangle beads. I sometimes like to substitute the 10° Triangle beads for the 8° seed beads, they add a bit more sparkle. You can use any of Miyuki white beads of your choice. They have lots of different whites. Or how about mixing in different colors as some of the samples in the books show. Be as creative as you want to be.

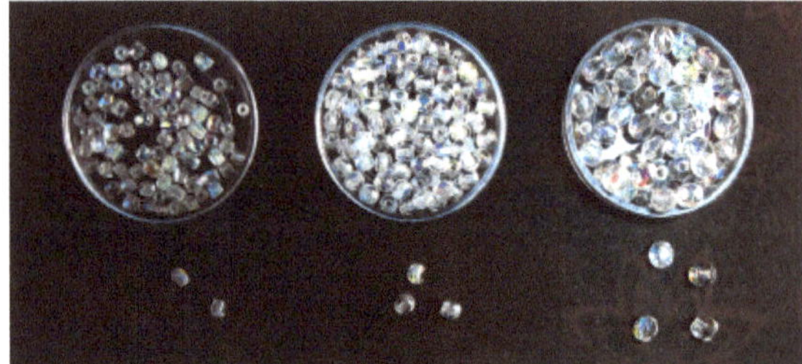

Fire-polish Glass Beads

In this book I use the Fire-polished crystals. I also use them for substituting some of the fancy shaped beads. These traditionally made beads are from the Czech Republic. The beads are shaped and faceted while hot, and then "fire-polished to smooth them. For this book I use 2mm, 3mm and 4mm crystals. Again as you can see, in some of the snowflake photos, your imagination of using different beads can be unlimited.

I have included a lot of snowflake ornament samples. Many of the snowflakes are made by Rose Young and Donna Lawson. Their samples are great because they show that you can use all kinds of colors, different shaped beads too. They have even used crystals and pearls. They are not afraid to just try different things. Use them as inspiration when making your snowflakes.

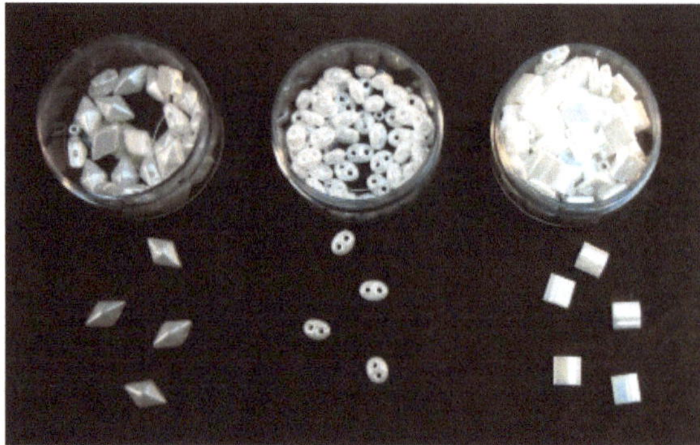

Fancy Beads

In this book, as an option for beads, I have used Tila beads, Twin Beads and DiamonDuo beads. These beads are optional and I have shown how to use the crystals or the fancy beads. You can use some, none or a combination of the beads.

Thread

What you would look for is a beading thread with a weight of D. My favorites are Nymo and C-Lon thread. This is a thread that is not too heavy and not too thin.

Match the color of thread to the color of beads that are in your project. I have recently started using the Fireline fishing line, too. I like 4lb and 6lb for bead weaving. You do not need to stretch or wax it.

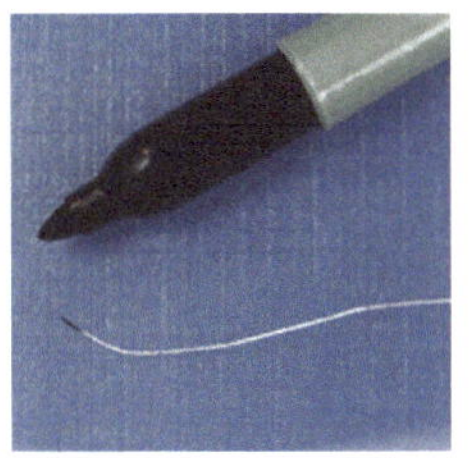

Whether using thread or fishing line, for ease in threading the beading needle use a marker and touch the tip of the thread. The marker makes the end of the thread more visible and it also stiffens the end of the thread. The thread will then go more easily into the needle hole.

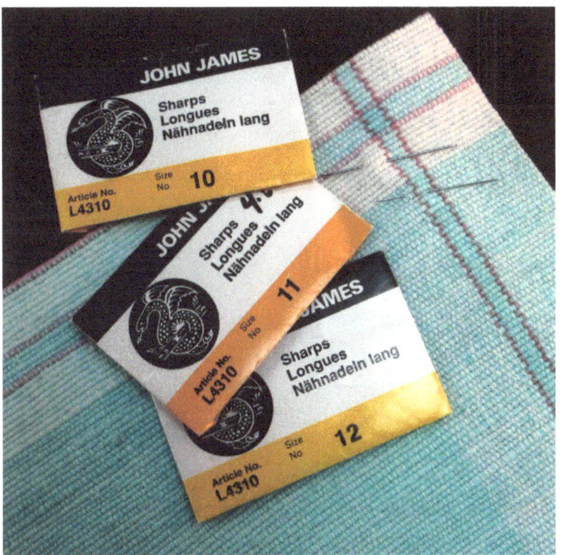

Needles

Beading needles come in different lengths and sizes. You will need sizes #11 and #12 beading needles. They come in short and long versions. I use the John James sharps. I prefer the short, but it really makes no difference if you use either one.

Beeswax

Beeswax is used for conditioning your thread. It can also help to keep your thread from tangling. You can get it from any beading store. Fabric stores also sell beeswax in a round plastic container.

White Glue

Glue is used for holding your knots and your thread in place. You will only need a touch of the glue. Put a dot of glue on the thread and spread the glue along the thread before weaving it into the snowflake. Be careful not to use too much, you just need a tiny bit. Note: If you are using dyed beads, check for color fastness before using the glue.

Scissors

You will need a small, very sharp scissors. Invest in a good pair; it is worth it.

Please note: With the beaded snowflakes, if you plan to stiffen your snowflake after, you really do not need to add the glue. The stiffener that you use will hold your thread ends in place.

Working Surface

A bead mat is best for working with seed beads. The mat will hold your beads on the mat while working on your pattern. I first start with a lap desk. This is a flat board, about 12" x 10", Cut a piece of no-slip vinyl shelf liner to fit (this keeps the tray in place, even if you have to get up really fast) and put that on the lap desk. Next, add a tray. You do not want the tray to have edges that are too high; otherwise, it will bother your arm if you are working on your lap. Then add another piece of shelf liner and finally a place-mat. I use a tightly-woven place-mat, so the beads don't get lost in the texture of the fabric. It also keeps the beads from bouncing at you when you are working. If I am working at a table, I just use the tray part, but if I am working on my lap, I use the whole set up.

A lot of people like using foam blanket material called Vellux to lay their beads on. I don't really like that stuff, I find my beads jump at me too much. I really like using a tightly woven place mat. You could also use a piece of felt. Really it is best to use whatever you are the most comfortable working with. You can experiment until you find what you like best.

Terminology

These are the terms that I use.

Pick up 4W, 1C, 3W

PICK UP

Pick up, is used for the amount and type of beads that you pick up on your working needle and thread. The picture above shows, Pick up 4A, 1B, 3A.

Go with thread

Go with thread refers to your working thread and needle.

I bring the needle to the beads on the tray when picking up, not the beads to the needle. The little silver spoon I use for scooping up beads to put them away.

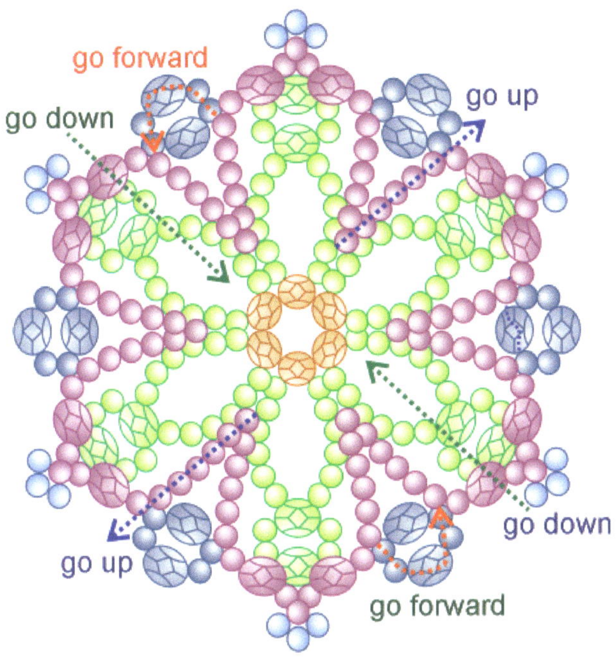

go forward
go up
go down

Go forward (counter-clockwise), is to go with your working thread and needle in the same direction as all the steps have gone. Go up, is to go toward the outside of the snowflake and go down, is to go down toward the center of the snowflake.

To Start

Cut about 1 yard of thread. When you get more experienced, you can start with a longer thread. When you cut the thread, cut it at an angle. This makes it easier to thread into the needle.

Run the thread through the beeswax a couple of times. Then run the thread through your fingers and stretch the thread as you are rubbing off the excess wax. DO NOT skip the stretching of the thread part. This is a big mistake that beginners make, including myself when I began. What can happen if you don't stretch the thread, after a while the thread will start to stretch on its own with the weight of the beads and the tension will become too loose. As you are working, keep in mind your tension.

You don't want the tension too tight, but you also don't want to see the thread.

Please Note: If you are using a fishing line, you do not need to wax or stretch it. Thread your beading needle. Hint: Pinch the thread between your thumb and finger. Then bring the thread to the needle hole. Beading needle holes are very small, so it takes a bit of patience when you first start to thread them.

Now you need to add a stopper bead to the end of the working thread. I use an overhand knot, so the bead will hold, but will also slide off easily. This bead can be a different color. The stopper bead is used to hold your beads on while you work on your piece and helps to keep your tension.

Pick up the stopper bead, slide it down to the end of your working thread, leaving at least an 8" tail. With the thread, make a loop over your stopper bead bringing the left end thread over and through the back of the right hand thread. Pull up ends so the thread is snug around the stopper bead.

When you are done, you can pull off the stopper bead by putting the blunt end of your needle through the bead and pull it off by sliding down the thread tail.

Bringing in new thread, and ending the old thread

When you start to run out of thread or if you see that your working thread is starting to fray, it is time to bring a new thread in and end the old thread.

The light blue line in the diagram at right represents the finished working thread. Go with thread back through several beads in your bead weaving. Make a half hitch knot (shown in diagram as light blue dots). Weave through several more beads again with your working thread and make another half hitch knot, but before pulling up the thread to tighten the knot, put a bit of the clear nail polish or clear glue on the knot area and about 1/4" along the thread. Please note though, with the beaded snowflakes, if you plan to stiffen your snowflake after, you really do not need to add the glue. The stiffener that you use will hold your thread ends in place. Pull up the knot tight and continue with the working thread through several more beads in your piece. Trim off the thread as close as possible to the beads.

Please note: If you make a knot, and you need to go through the bead where the knot is, the bead hole will be blocked. You can go back later to do the knotting. You never want to force the needle though beads, the beads are made of glass and can be broken.

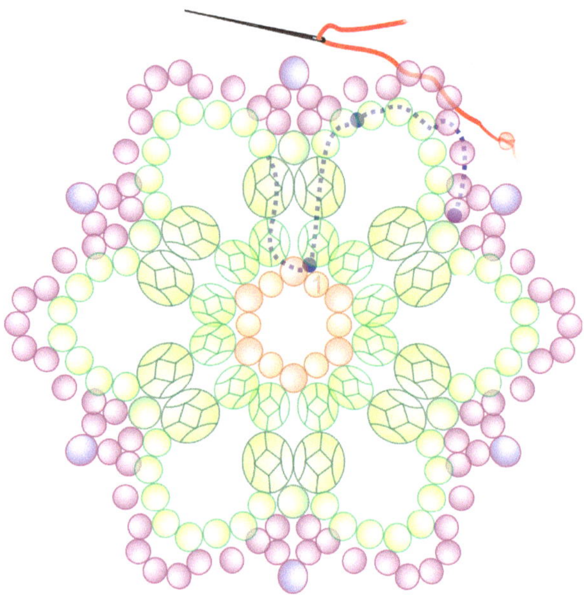

The red line in the diagram represents bringing in a new thread with a stopper bead. The stopper bead can be removed after several steps have been completed in the pattern. Pull off the stopper bead and weave off the end of the new thread in the opposite direction of the old thread.

The Half Hitch Knot

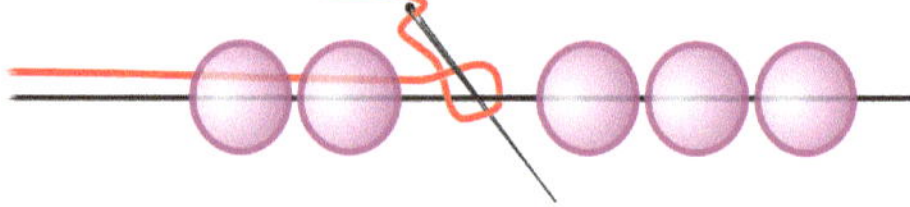

To make a half hitch knot, go around the thread in the piece with your working thread and needle between 2 beads. Make a loop and go through the loop in the working thread, pull up to tighten. Please note: When weaving your threads through areas that have already been done, try not to split the threads with your working needle as it can weaken your threads.

Bead colors for Rounds

R = Round

 Each Round begins at the red dot in the illustration. All of the snowflakes are done in Rounds. The Rounds are normally worked counter-clockwise unless otherwise noted.

Throughout this book the same colors are used for the Rounds as shown below.

- Round 1
- Round 2
- Round 3
- Round 4
- Round 5
- Round 6
- Round 7
- Round 8

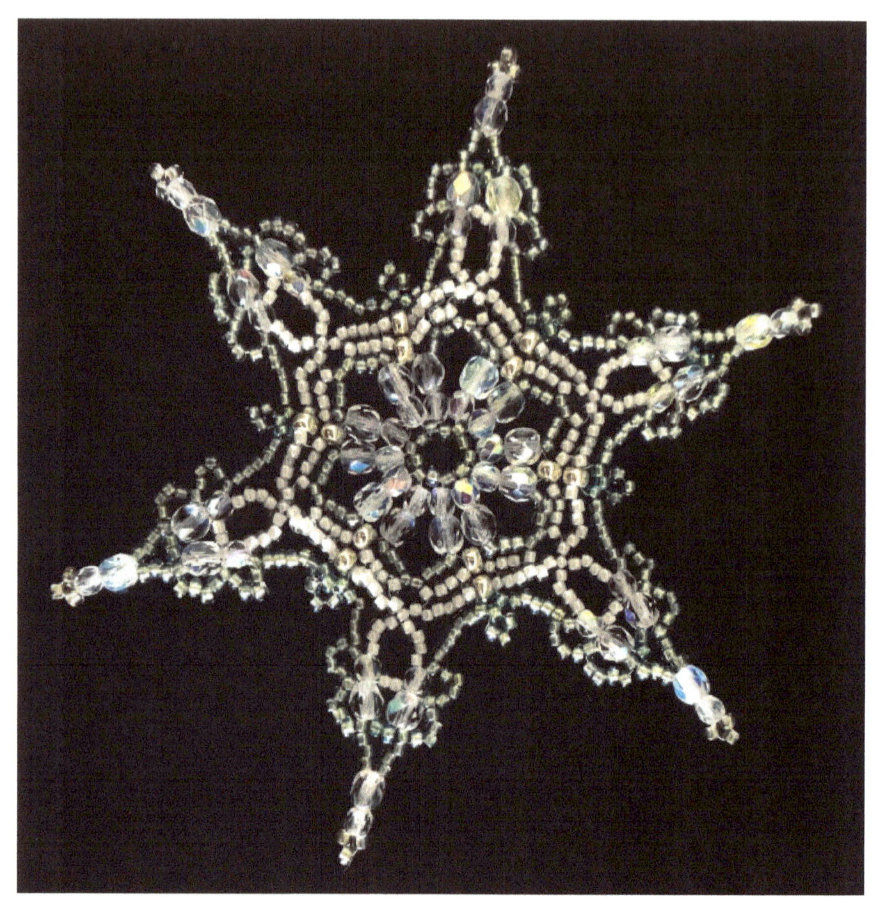

Blazing Snowflake Ornament

Dazzling Snowflake Ornament

Ablaze Snowflake Ornament
2-3/4 Inches

One Version
A = Miyuki 11° SEED bead,
720 beads
F = Miyuki 15° SEED bead,
12 beads

Round 1

Pick up 12A, go with thread forward through the 1st A bead. Continue with thread around through all 12 A beads again coming out with thread at the 1st A bead.

Round 2

a) Pick up 7A, go with thread forward through the same bead that your working thread in exiting and continue forward through 2 more A beads in R1.

b) Repeat (a) around 5 more times.

c) Continue with working thread forward through the 1st and 2nd A beads added in the first repeat of (a) this Round.

Round 2

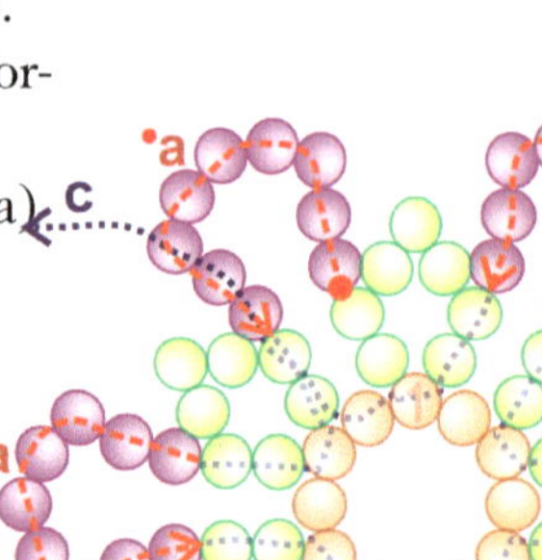

Round 3

Round 3

a) Pick up 9A, go with thread down through the 6th and 7th A beads, R2a, right to left through 1 A bead in R1, and up through the 1st and 2nd A beads, R2a.

b) Repeat (a) around 5 more times, ending at the last repeat going with working thread through 2 A beads in R1 as shown.

c) Continue with working thread up through the 9th, 8th and 7th A beads added in the first repeat of (a) this Round.

Round 4

a) Pick up 7A, go with thread down through the 3rd A bead, R3a.

b) Pick up 1F, go with thread left to right through the 4th A bead, R2a.

c) Pick up 1F, go with thread up through the 7th A bead, R3a, and the 1st, 2nd and 3rd A beads added in this Round at (a).

d) Pick up 8A, go with thread forward through the 5th A bead just added in this step.

e) Pick up 6A, go with thread forward through the 1st A bead just added in this step.

f) Pick up 4A, go with thread forward through the 1st A bead just added in this step.

g) Pick up 4A, go with thread down through the 5th, 6th and 7th A beads added in this Round at (a), the 3rd, 2nd and 1st A beads, R3a, and up through the 9th, 8th and 7th A beads, R3a.

h) Repeat (a, b, c, d, e, f, g) around 5 more times.

i) After adding the A beads in the last repeat of (g), continue with working thread forward through the A beads added in this Round at (a) and right to left through the 4th A bead, R3a.

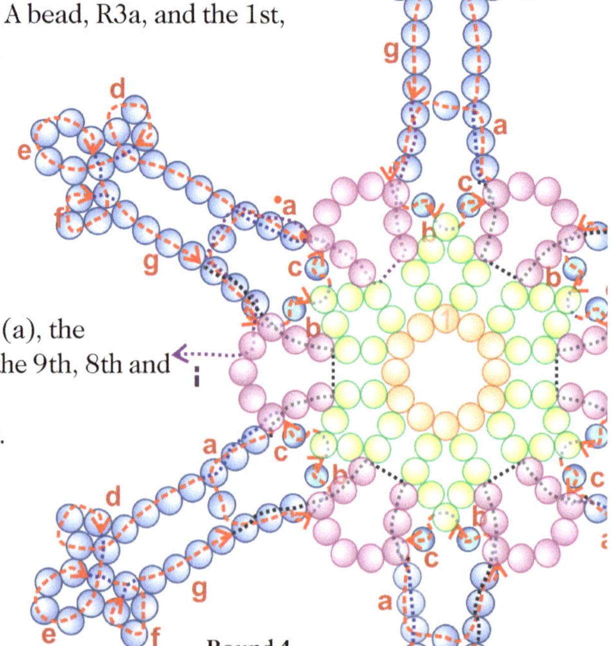

Round 4

Round 5

a) Pick up 4A, go with thread down through the 5th, 6th and 7th A beads, R4a, and right to left through the 4th and 5th A beads, R3a.

b) Pick up 6A, go with thread down through the 3rd, 2nd and 1st A beads added at (a), and right to left through the 5th and 6th A beads, R3a, and up through the 1st, 2nd and 3rd A beads, R4a.

c) Pick up 1A, go with thread down through the 3rd, 2nd and 1st A beads added at (b), right to left through the 6th and 7th A beads, R3a, the F bead, R4c, the 4th A bead, R2a, the F bead, R4b, and the 3rd and 4th A beads, R3a.

d) Repeat (a, b, c) around 5 more times.

e) Continue with working thread up through the 4 A beads, R4g, and the 1st, 4th and 3rd A beads, R4f.

Round 6

a) Pick up 6A, go with thread right to left through the 6th A bead, R5b.

b) Pick up 3A, go with thread down through the 3rd, 2nd and 1st A beads added at (a), right to left through the 6th and 5th A beads, R5b, and up through the 3 A beads just added.

c) Pick up 4A, go with thread forward through the 1st A bead just added.

d) Pick up 3A, go with thread right to left through the 4th A bead, R5b.

e) Pick up 3A, go with thread down through the 3 A beads added at (d), right to left through the 4th A bead, R5b, and up through the 3 A beads just added.

f) Pick up 3A, go with thread up through the 7th A bead, R4d.

g) Pick up 5A, go with thread forward through the 2nd A bead just added.

h) Pick up 1A, go with thread right to left through the 4th A bead, R4e.

i) Pick up 3A, go with thread right to left through the 4th A bead, R4e, and forward through the 1st and 2nd A beads just added.

j) Pick up 3A, go with thread forward through the 2nd A bead added in the last step and forward through the 1st and 2nd A beads just added.

k) Pick up 3A, go with thread forward through the 2nd and 3rd A beads added in the last step, the second and 3rd A beads added at (i) and the 4th A bead, R4e.

l) Pick up 5A, go with thread forward through the 2nd A bead just added.

m) Pick up 1A, go with thread down through the 3rd A bead, R4f.

n) Repeat (a, b, c, d, e, f, g, h, i, j, k, l, m) around 5 more times.

o) Weave the working thread into the snowflake and end.

Radiance Snowflake Ornament
3 Inches

Version 1
A = Miyuki 11° SEED bead,
    700 beads
B = 3 mm crystals,
    6 crystals

Version 2
A = Miyuki 11° SEED bead,
    700 beads
D = DiamonDuo Beads,
    12 beads

Round 1 - V1 and V2

Pick up 12A, go with thread forward through the 1st A bead. Continue with thread around through all 12 A beads again coming out with thread at the 1st A bead.

Round 2 - V1 and V2

a) Pick up 3A, go with thread down through the 2nd and 1st A beads just added in this step and forward through the next 2 A beads in R1.

b) Repeat (a) around 5 more times.

c) Continue with working thread forward through the 1st, 2nd and 3rd A beads added in the first repeat of (a) this Round.

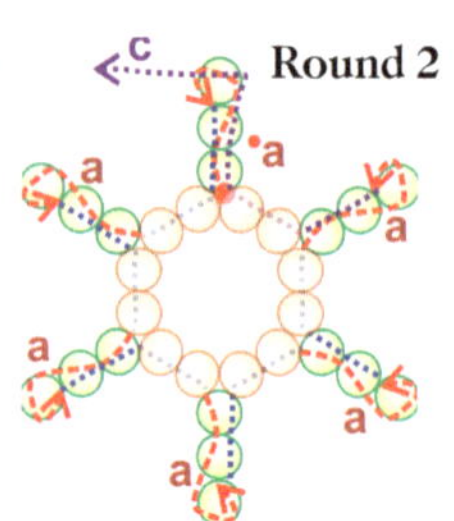

Round 3 - V1 and V2

a) Pick up 22A, go with thread right to left through the 3rd A bead, R2a, and forward through the 1st through 11th A bead just added in this step.

b) Pick up 1A, go with thread forward through the 12 through 22nd A beads, this Round at (a), right to left through the 3rd A bead and down through the 2nd A bead, R2a.

c) Pick up 3A, go with thread up through the 2nd A bead and right to left through the 3rd A bead, R2a.

d) Repeat (a, b, c) around 5 more times.

e) Continue with working thread forward through the 1st through 6th A beads added in the first repeat of (a) this Round.

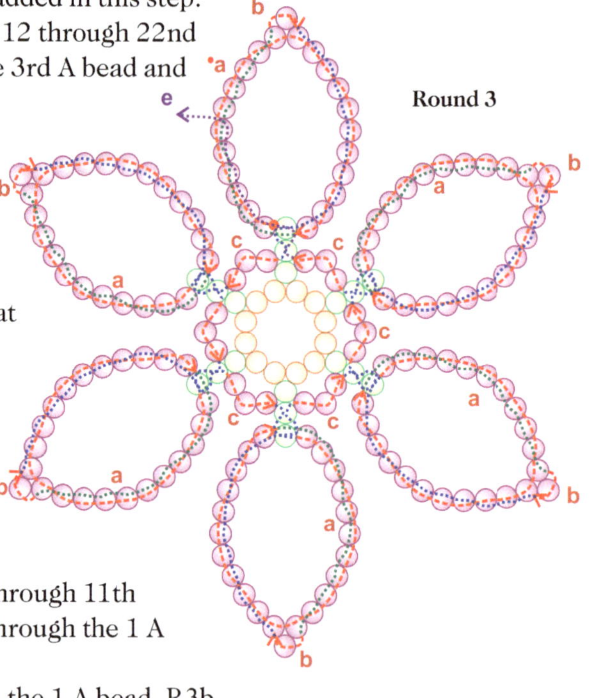

Round 4 - V1
This Round is worked Clockwise

a) Pick up 5A, go with thread down through the 17th and 18th A beads, R3a.

b) Pick up 1B, go with thread up through the 5th through 11th A beads, R3a, repeat to the right and left to right through the 1 A bead, R3b.

c) Pick up 10A, go with thread left to right through the 1 A bead, R3b and the 1st through 5th A beads just added in this step.

d) Pick up 1A, go with thread forward through the 6th through 10th A beads, R4c, left to right through the 1 A bead, R3b, down through the 12th through 18th A beads, R3a.

e) Pick up 1B, go with thread up through the 5th and 6th A beads, R3a, repeat to the right.

f) Pick up 5A, go with thread down through the 17th and 18th A beads, R3a, left to right through the 1 B bead, R4b, or the 1 B bead, R4e, up through the 5th through 11th A beads, R3a, repeat to the right and left to right through the 1 A bead, R3b.

g) Repeat (c, d, e, f) around 4 more times. Repeat (c, d*) one time.

h) *At the last repeat of (d) go with thread forward through the 6th through 10th A beads, R4c, left to right through the 1 A bead, R3b. Continue with working thread through the snowflake coming out with thread forward (up) through the 1st, 2nd, 3rd and 4th A beads, R4c. If you get confused just follow the thread path in illustration.

Round 4 - V2

This Round is worked Clockwise

a) Pick up 2A, 1D, 2A, go with thread down through the 17th and 18th A beads, R3a.

b) Pick up 1A, go with thread left to right through the bottom hole of the D bead added in the last step. Pick up 1A, go with thread up through the 5th through 11th A beads, R3a, repeat to the right and left to right through the 1 A bead, R3b.

c) Pick up 10A, go with thread left to right through the 1 A bead, R3b and the 1st through 5th A beads just added in this step.

d) Pick up 1A, go with thread forward through the 6th through 10th A beads, R4c, left to right through the 1 A bead, R3b and down through the 12th through 18th A beads, R3a.

e) Pick up 1A, 1D, 1A, go with thread up through the 5th and 6th A beads, R3a, repeat to the right.

f) Pick up 2A, go with thread right to left through the top hole of the D bead, R4e. Pick up 2A, go with thread down through the 17th and 18th A beads, R3a, left to right through the 1 A, 1 D and 1 A bead, R4e, up through the 5th through 11th A beads, R3a, repeat to the right and left to right through the 1 A bead, R3b.

g) Repeat (c, d, e, f) around 4 more times. Repeat (c, d*) one time.

h) *At the last repeat of (d) go with thread forward through the 6th through 10th A beads, R4c, left to right through the 1 A bead, R3b. Continue with working thread through the snowflake coming out with thread forward (up) through the 1st, 2nd, 3rd and 4th A beads, R4c. If you get confused just follow the thread path in illustration.

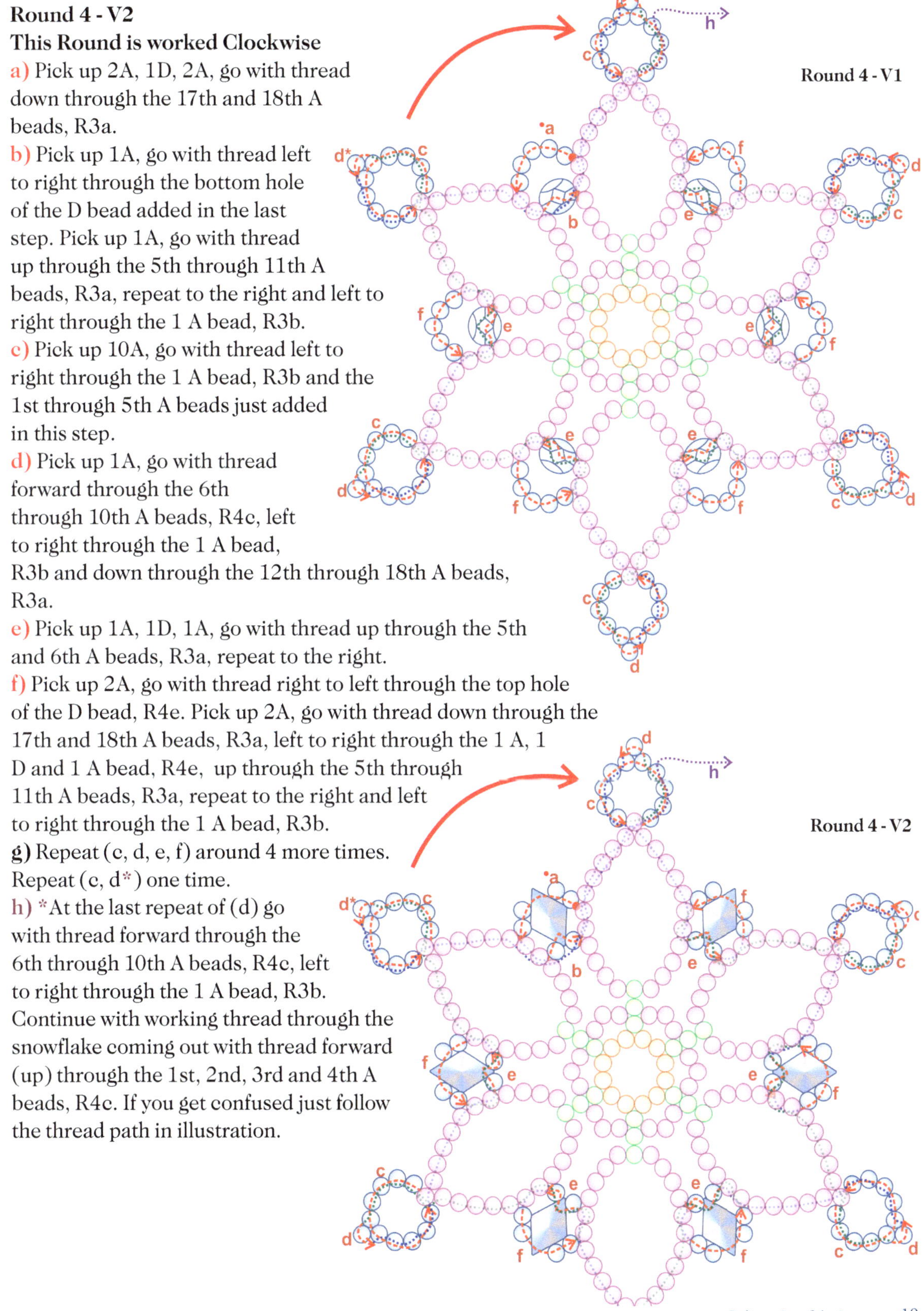

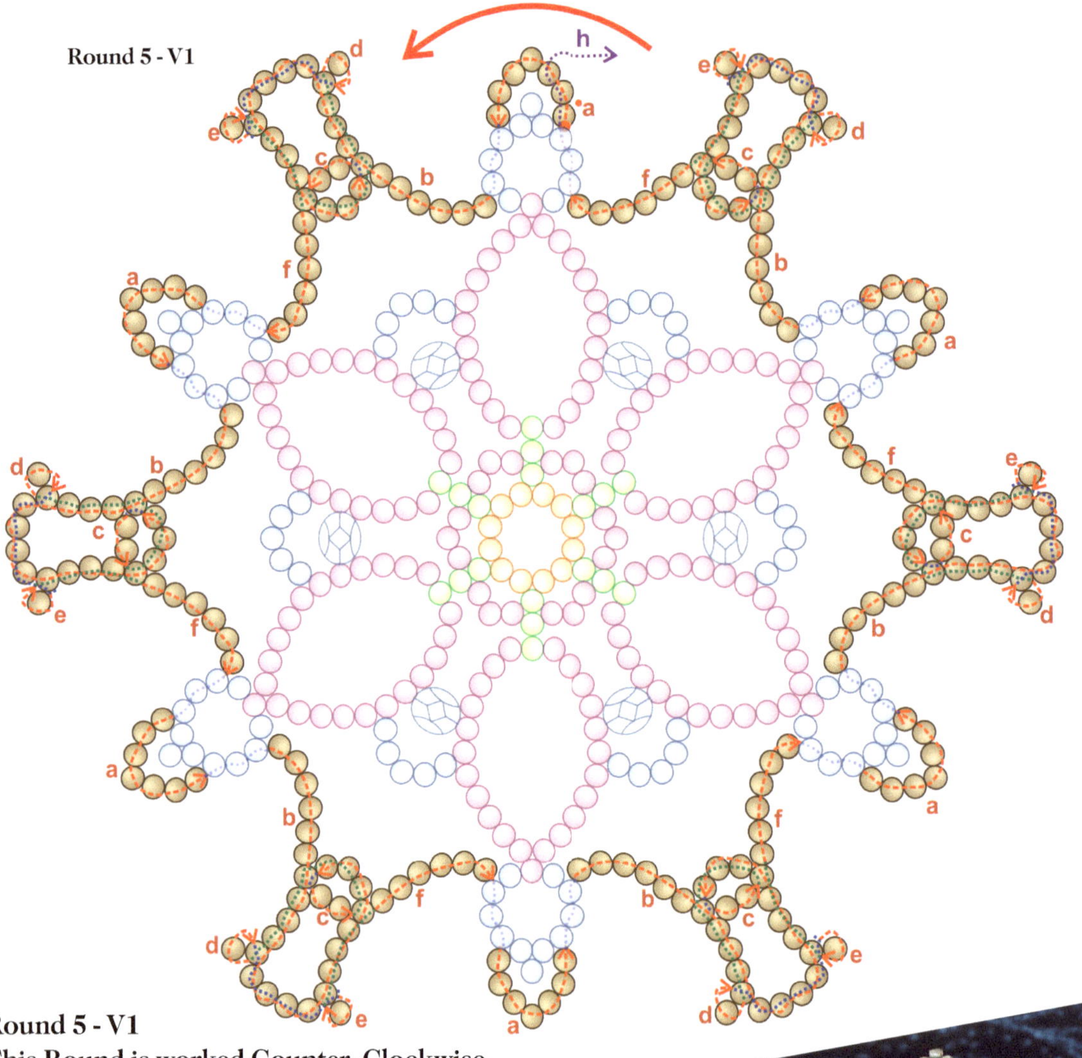

Round 5 - V1
This Round is worked Counter- Clockwise

a) Pick up 7A, go with thread down through the 7th, 8th and 9th A beads, R4c.

b) Pick up 13A, go with thread up through the 7th A bead just added.

c) Pick up 5A, go with thread forward through the 4th A bead just added.

d) Pick up 6A, go with thread forward through the 5th A bead just added.

e) Pick up 3A, go with thread down through the 10th A bead, this Round at (b)

f) Pick up 6A, go with thread up through the 2nd, 3rd and 4th A beads, R4c.

g) Repeat (a, b, c, d, e, f) around 5 more times.

h) Continue with working thread up through the 1st, 2nd and 3rd A beads added in the first Repeat of (a) in this Round.

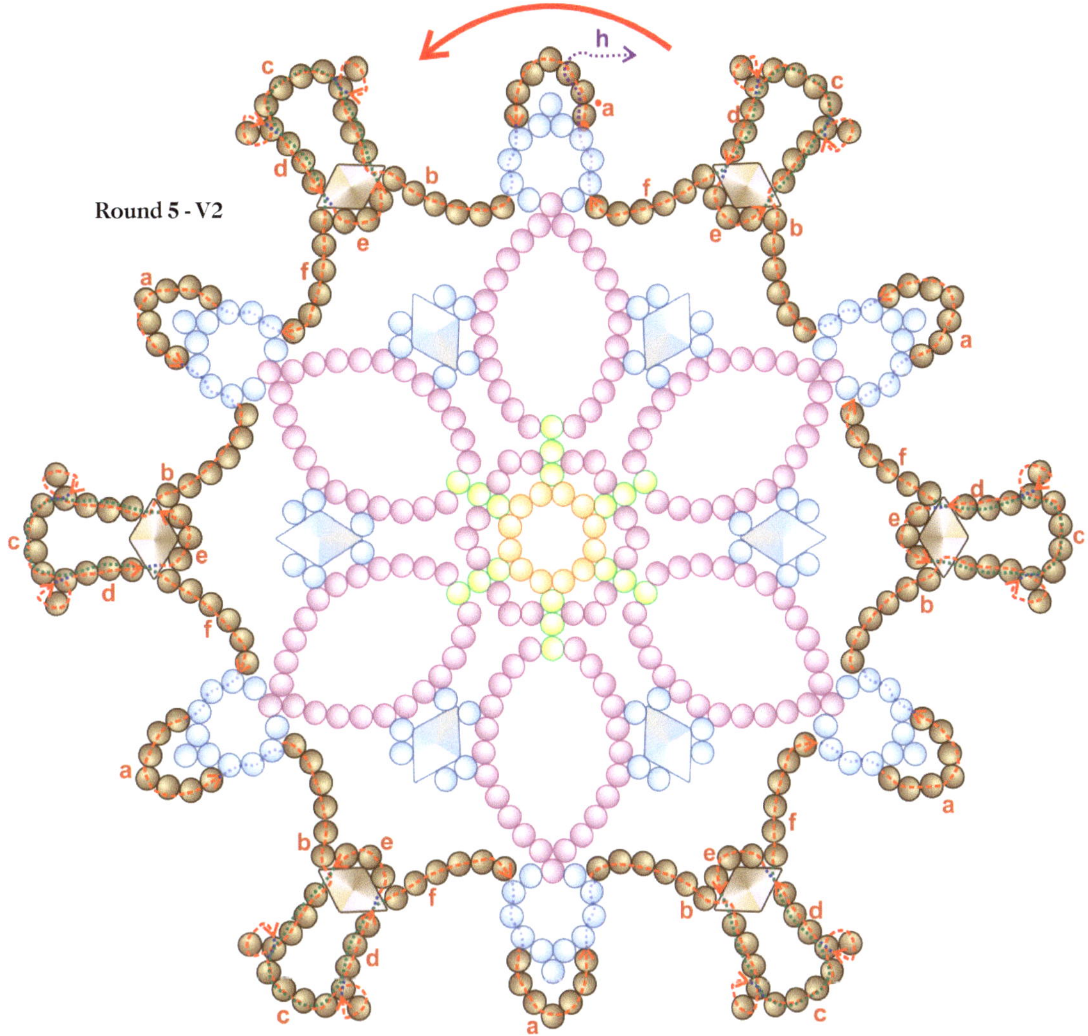

Round 5 - V2
This Round is worked Counter- Clockwise
a) Pick up 7A, go with thread down through the 7th, 8th and 9th A beads, R4c.
b) Pick up 6A, 1D, 5A, go with thread forward through the 4th A bead just added.
c) Pick up 6A, go with thread forward through the 5th A bead just added.
d) Pick up 3A, go with thread down through the left side hole of the D bead added at (b).
e) Pick up 3A, go with thread up and then forward through the D bead and the 1st, 2nd, 3rd and 4th A beads (of the 5A), the 1st through 5th A beads, this round at (c), the 3 A beads added in this Round at (d) and the left side hole of the D bead added at (b).
f) Pick up 6A, go with thread up through the 2nd, 3rd and 4th A beads, R4c.
g) Repeat (a, b, c, d, e, f) around 5 more times.
h) Continue with working thread up through the 1st, 2nd and 3rd A beads added in the first Repeat of (a) in this Round.

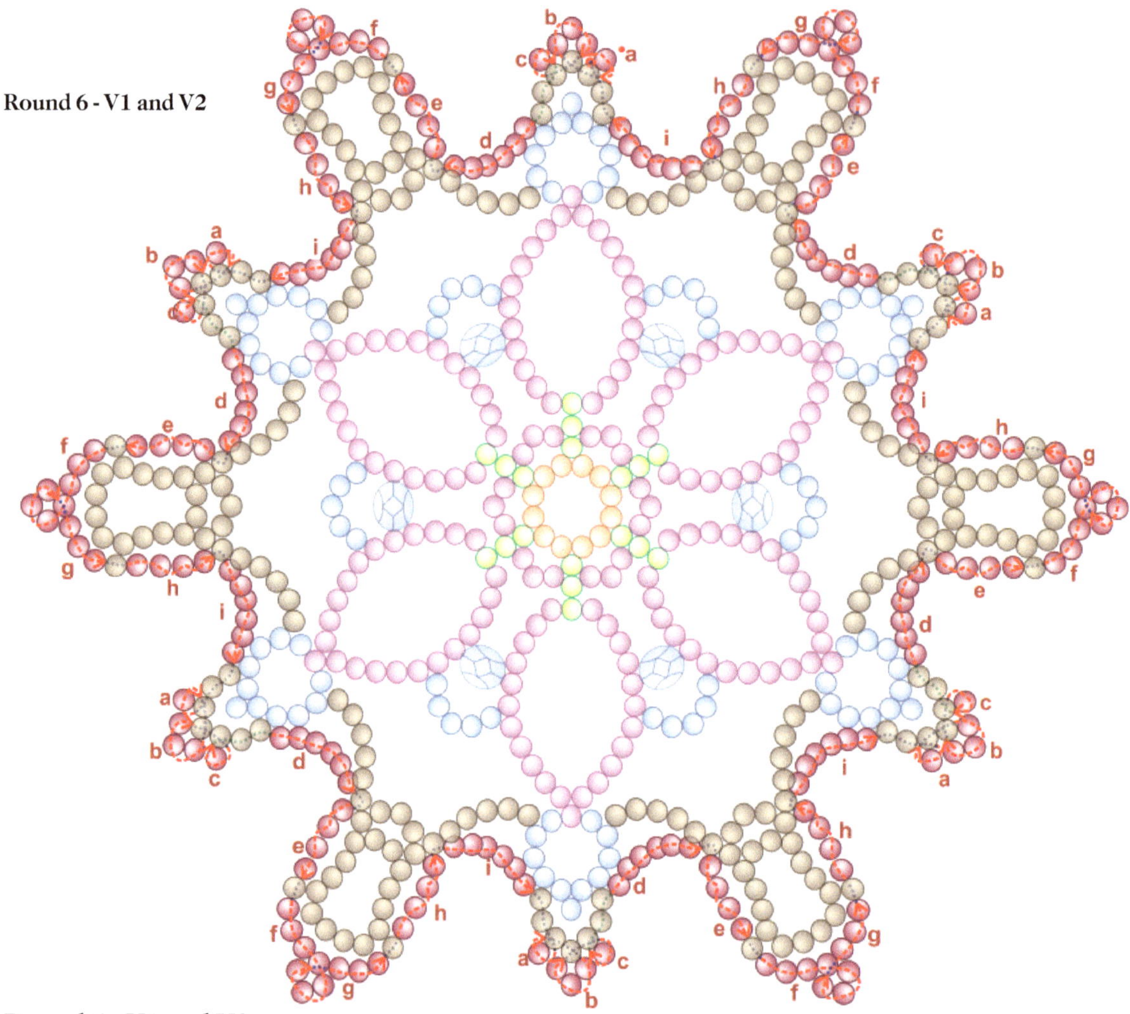

Round 6 - V1 and V2

a) Pick up 1A, go with thread forward through the 3rd and 4th A beads, R5a.

b) Pick up 3A, go with thread forward through the 4th and 5th A beads, R5a.

c) Pick up 1A, go with thread forward through the 5t h, 6th and 7th A beads, R5a.

d) Pick up 4A* (V-1) or 6A* (V-2), go with thread up through the 6th A bead, R5b-v1 or the 5th A bead, R5b-v2.

e) Pick up 4A*, go with thread up through the 5th A bead, R5c-v1 or the 5th A bead (of the 5 A), R5b-v2.

f) Pick up 7A, go with thread forward through the 4th A bead just added.

g) Pick up 3A, go with thread down through the 6th A bead, R5d-v1 or the 6th A bead, R5c-v2.

h) Pick up 4A*, go with thread down through the 1st A bead, R5f.

i) Pick up 4A* (V-1) or 6A* (V-2), go with thread up through the 1st, 2nd and 3rd A beads, R5a.

j) Repeat (a, b, c, d, e, f, g, h, i) around 5 more times.

k) Weave the working thread into the snowflake and end.

*IN V-1, depending on the type of seed beads you are using, you can try 5A instead of 4A. Adding 4A beads is a bit tighter and using the 5A beads is a bit looser. You can experiment with either V1 or V2 and the amount of beads you add in this step..

Brilliant Snowflake Ornament
3-1/4 Inches

One Version
A = Miyuki 11° SEED bead,
   600 beads
B = 3 mm Fire-polished crystals,
   12 crystals

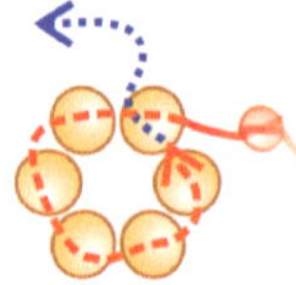

Round 1

Pick up 6A, go with thread forward through the 1st A bead. Continue with thread around through all 6 A beads again coming out with thread at the 1st A bead.

Round 2

a) Pick up 2A, go with thread down through the 1st A bead just added and forward through the next 1 A bead in R1.

b) Repeat (a) around 5 more times.

c) Continue with working thread forward through the 1st and 2nd A beads added in the first repeat of (a) this Round.

Round 3

Round 2

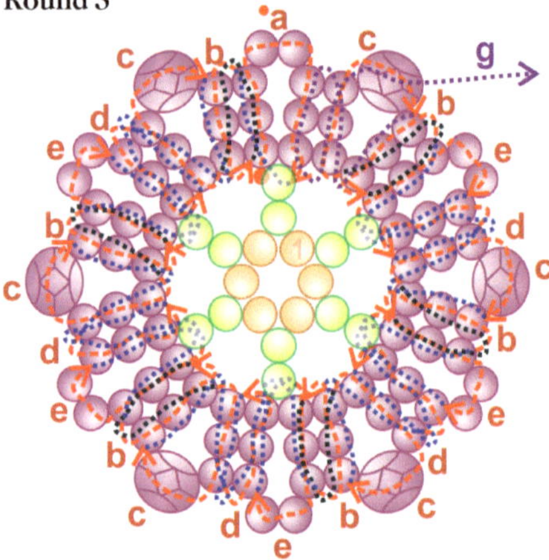

Round 3

Round 3

a) Pick up 8A, go with thread right to left through the 2nd A bead, R2a, and up through the 1st, 2nd and 3rd A beads just added in this step.

b) Pick up 3A, go with thread up through the 1st, 2nd and 3rd A beads, added in this Round at (a) or (e) and down through the 3 A beads just added in this step.

c) Pick up 3A, 1B, go with thread down through the 1st, 2nd and 3rd A beads added in this Round at (b) and up through the 1st, 2nd and 3rd A beads just added in this step.

d) Pick up 3A, go with thread up through the 1st, 2nd and 3rd A beads, added in this Round at (c) and down through the 3 A beads just added in this step, and right to left through the 2nd A bead, R2.

e) Pick up 5A, go with thread down through the 3 A beads added in this Round at (d), right to left through the 2nd A bead, R2, and up through the 1st, 2nd and 3rd A beads just added in this step.

f) Repeat (b, c, d, e) around 4 more times. Repeat (b, c) 1 more time.

g) Continue with working thread down through the 6th, 7th and 8th A beads, this Round at (a), up through the 1st, 2nd, and 3rd A beads, and left to right though the B bead added in this Round at the last repeat of (c).

Round 4

This Round is worked Clockwise

a) Pick up 2A, go with thread left to right through the 4th A bead, R3e.

b) Pick up 3A, go with thread down through the 2nd and 1st A beads just added in this step and left to right through the 5th A bead, R3e.

c) Pick up 2A, go with thread left to right through the 1 B bead, R3c.

d) Repeat (a, b, c) around 5 more times.

e) Continue with working thread up through the 3 A beads added in the first repeat of (b) in this round.

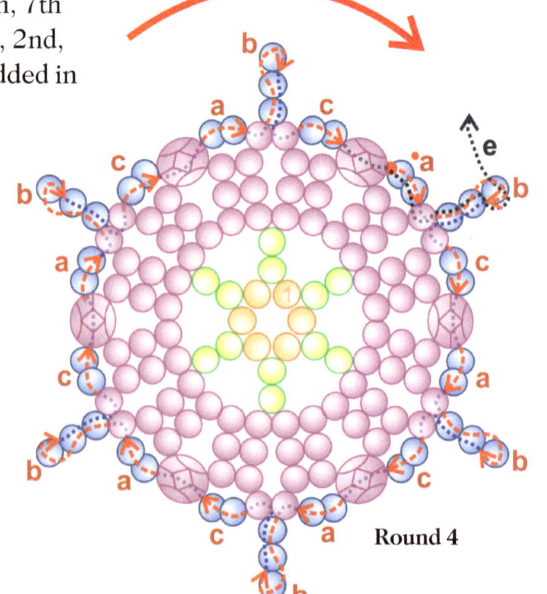

Round 4

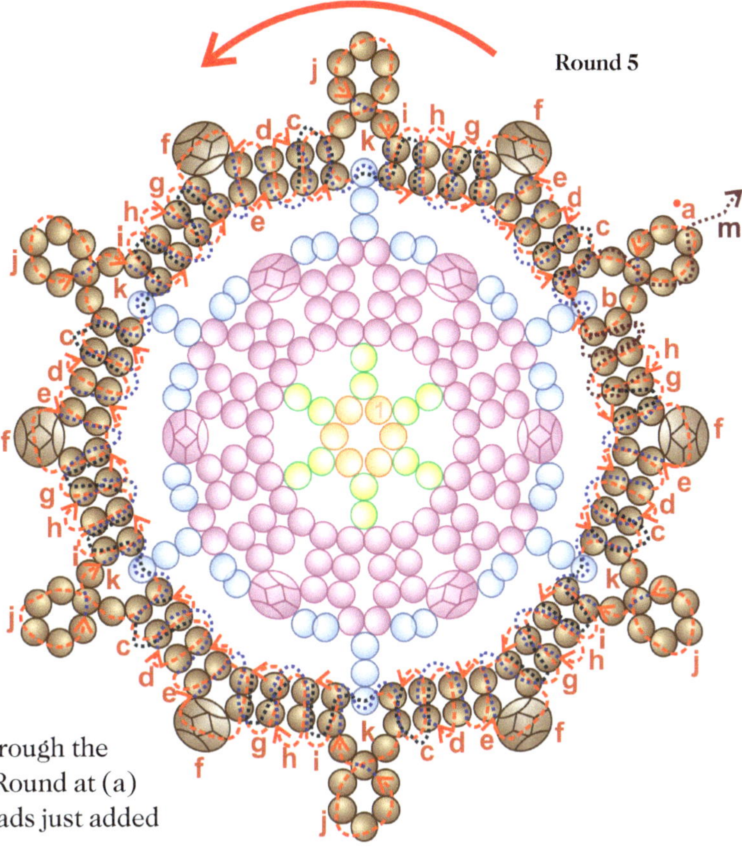

Round 5
This Round is worked Counter - Clockwise

a) Pick up 9A, go with thread forward through the 4th A bead just added in this step.

b) Pick up 3A, go with thread right to left through the 3rd A bead, R4b and up through the 1st and 2nd A beads added this round at (a).

c) Pick up 2A, go with thread up through the 1st and 2nd A beads added in this Round at (a) or (j) and down through the 2 A beads just added in this step.

d) Pick up 2A, go with thread down through the 2 A beads added in this Round at (c) and up through the 2 A beads just added in this step.

e) Pick up 2A, go with thread up through the 2 A beads added in this Round at (d) and down through the 2 A beads just added in this step.

f) Pick up 2A, 1B, go with thread down through the 2 A beads added in this Round at (e) and up through the 2 A beads just added in this step.

g) Pick up 2A, go with thread up through the 2 A beads added in this Round at (f) and down through the 2 A beads just added in this step.

h) Pick up 2A, go with thread down through the 2 A beads added in this Round at (g) and up through the 2 A beads just added in this step.

i) Pick up 2A, go with thread up through the 2 A beads added in this Round at (h), down through the 2 A beads just added in this step and right to left through the 3rd A bead, R4b.

j) Pick up 9A, go with thread forward through the 4th A bead just added in this step.

k) Pick up 1A, go with thread down through the 2 A beads, added in this Round at (i), right to left through the 3rd A bead, R4b and up through the 1st and 2nd A beads added in this Round at (j).

l) Repeat (c, d, e, f, g, h, i, j, k) around 4 more times.

Repeat (c, d, e, f, g, h) 1 more time.

m) After adding the beads in the last repeat of (h) go with working thread down through the 2nd and 3rd A beads added in this Round at (b), up through the 2 A beads this Round at (h), down through the 2nd and 3rd A beads, this Round at (b), right to left through the 3rd A bead, R4b, and up through the 1st, 2nd, 3rd, 4th, 5th, 6th and 7th A beads added at (a).

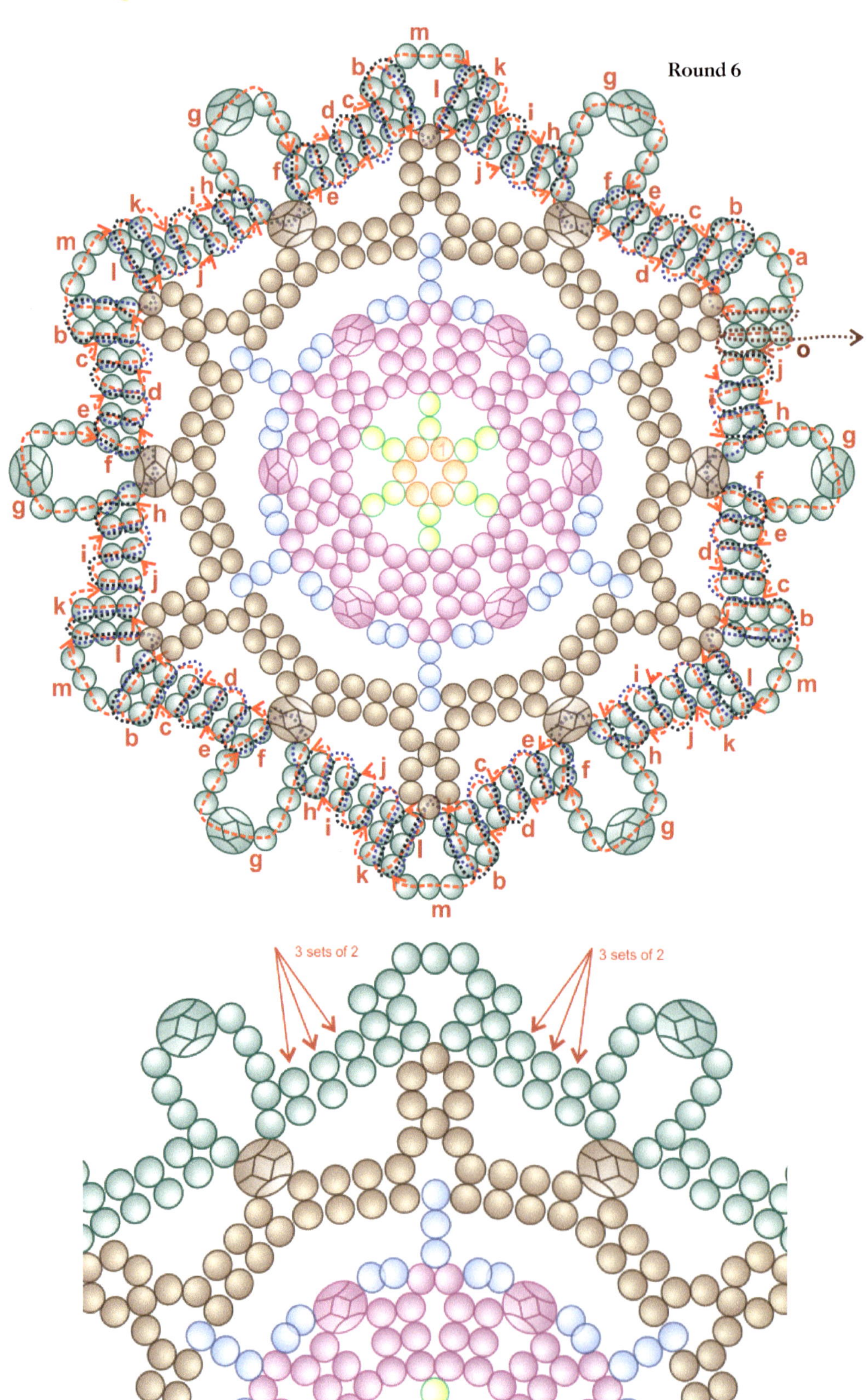
3 sets of 2
3 sets of 2

Round 6

a) Pick up 9A, go with thread right to left through the 7th A bead, R5a or R5j and up through the 1st, 2nd and 3rd A beads just added in this step.

b) Pick up 3A, go with thread up through the 1st, 2nd and 3rd A added at (a) or (m) and down through the 3 A beads just added in this step.

c) Pick up 2A, go with thread down through the 2nd and 3rd A beads added in this Round at (b) and up through the 2 A beads just added.

d) Pick up 2A, go with thread up through the 2 A beads added in this Round at (c) and down through the 2 A beads just added.

e) Pick up 2A, go with thread down through the 2 A beads added in this Round at (d) and up through the 2 A beads just added.

f) Pick up 2A, go with thread up through the 2 A beads added in this Round at (e), down through the 2 A beads just added and right to left through the B bead, R5f.

g) Pick up 5A, 1B, 3A, go with thread down through the 2 A beads added in this Round at (f), right to left through the B bead, R5f and up through the 1st and 2nd A beads added in this Round at (g).

h) Pick up 2A, go with thread up through the 1st and 2nd A beads added in this Round at (g) and down through the 2 A beads just added.

i) Pick up 2A, go with thread down through the 2 A beads added in this Round at (h) and up through the 2 A beads just added.

j) Pick up 2A, go with thread up through the 2 A beads added in this Round at (i) and down through the 2 A beads just added.

k) Pick up 3A, go with thread down through the 2 A beads added in this Round at (j) and up through the 3 A beads just added.

l) Pick up 3A, go with thread up through the 3 A beads added in this Round at (k), down through the 3 A beads just added and right to left through the 7th A bead, R5a or R5j.

m) Pick up 6A, go with thread down through the 3 A beads added at (l), right to left through the 7th A bead, R5a or R5j and up through the 1st, 2nd and 3rd A beads just added in this step.

n) Repeat (b, c, d, e, f, g, h, i, j, k, l, m) around 4 more times.
Repeat (b, c, d, e, f, g, h, i, j) 1 more time.

o) Pick up 3A, go with working thread down through the 2 A beads added at (j), up through the 3 A beads just added in this step, down through the 7th, 8th and 9th A beads added at (a) and up through the 3 A beads just added in this step.

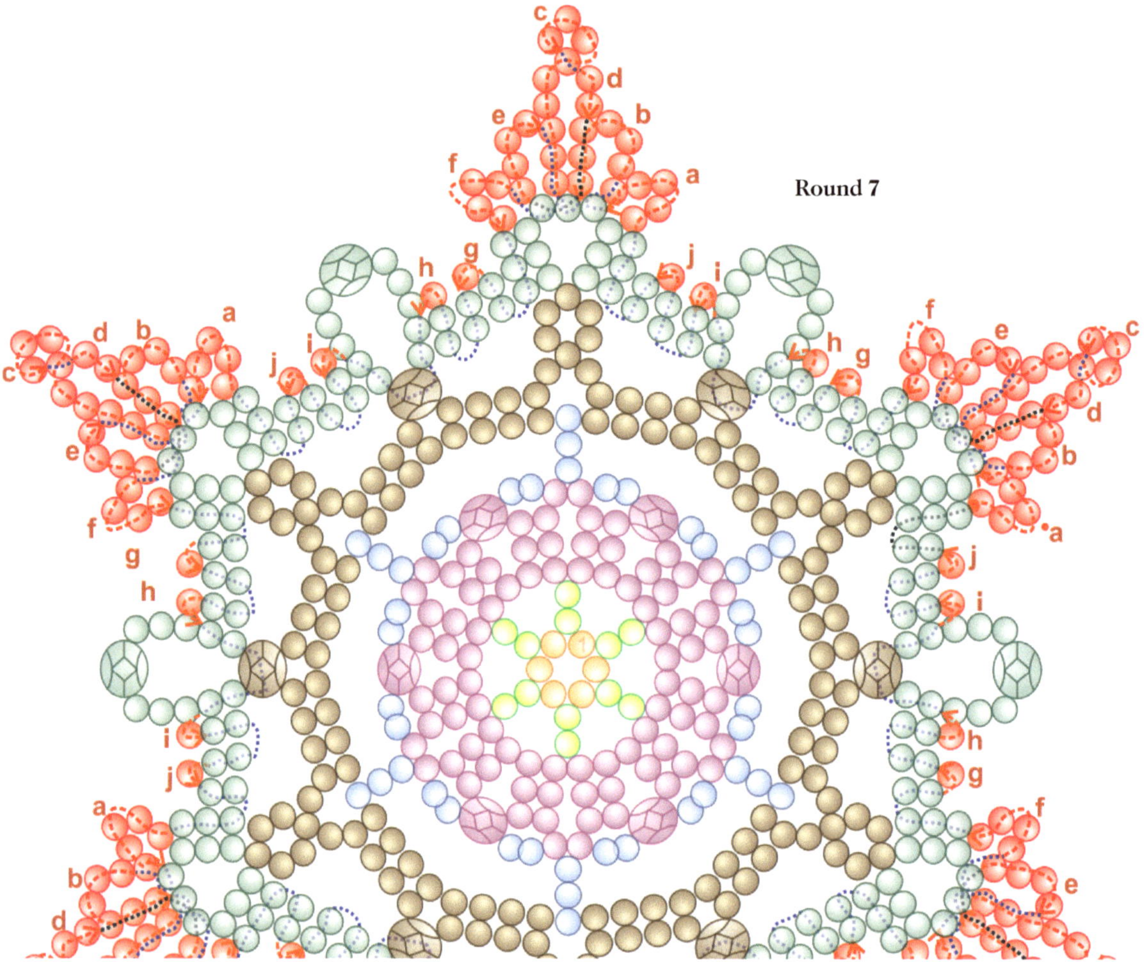

Round 7

a) Pick up 5A, go with thread right to left through the 6th A bead, R6a or R6m, and up through the 5th A bead just added in this step.

b) Pick up 6A, go with thread right to left through the 5th A bead, R6a or R6m.

c) Pick up 9A, go with thread forward through the 6th A bead just added in this step.

d) Pick up 2A, go with thread down through the 4th, 5th and 6th A beads added in this Round at (b) and right to left through the 5th and 4th A beads, R6a or R6m.

e) Pick up 4A, go with thread down through the 3rd, 2nd and 1st A beads added in this round at (c), right to left through the 4th A bead, R6a or R6m, and up through the 1st A bead just added in this step.

f) Pick up 4A, go with thread down through the 3 A beads, R6b, up through the 2 A beads, R6c.

g) Pick up 1A, go with thread down through the 2 A beads, R6d and up through the 2 A beads, R6e.

h) Pick up 1A, go with thread down through the 2 A beads, R6f, right to left through the B bead, R5f and up through the 2 A beads, R6g.

i) Pick up 1A, go with thread down through the 2 A beads, R6h and up through the 2 A beads, R6i.

j) Pick up 1A, go with thread down through the 2 A beads, R6j and up through the 3 A beads, R6k.

k) Repeat (a, b, c, d, e, f, g, h, i, j) around 5 more times.

l) Weave the working thread into the snowflake and end.

Blazing Snowflake Ornament

3 - 1/2 Inches

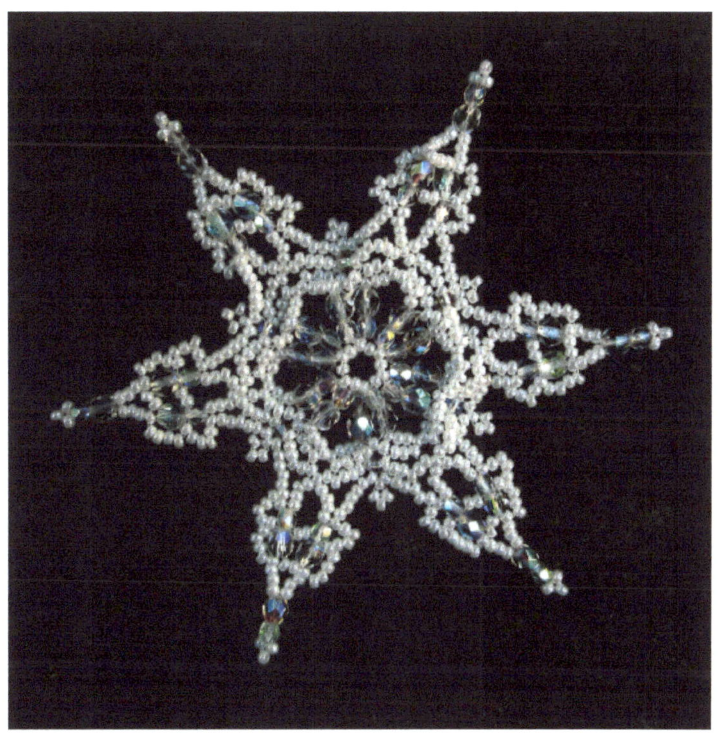

Version 1
A = Miyuki 11° SEED bead,
    550 beads
B = 3 mm crystals,
    30 crystals
C = 4 mm crystals,
    30 crystals
E = Miyuki 8° SEED bead,
    12 beads

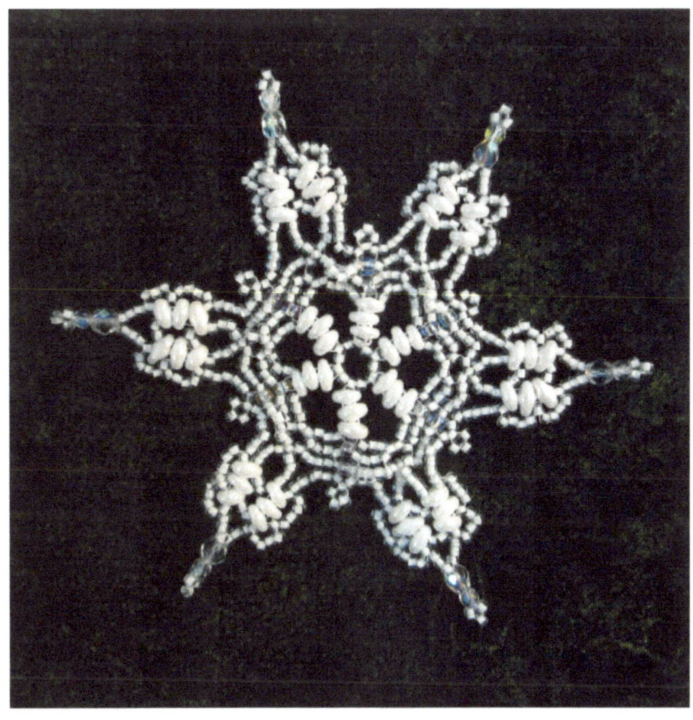

Version 2
A = Miyuki 11° SEED bead,
    550 beads
B = 3 mm crystals,
    6 crystals
C = 4 mm crystals,
    6 crystals
E = Miyuki 8° SEED bead,
    12 beads
W = Twin Beads,
    54 beads

Round 1 - V1 and V2

Pick up 12A, go with thread forward through the 1st A bead. Continue with thread around through all 12 A beads again coming out with thread at the 1st A bead.

Round 2 - V1

a) Pick up 1B, 1C, 1E, 1C, 1B, go with thread right to left through 1A bead in R1, and up through the 1st B and 1st C beads.

b) Pick up 8A, 1C, 1 B, go with thread right to left through 1A bead in R1 as shown.

c) Pick up 1B, 1C, 1E, go with thread down through the 1 C and 1 B beads added at (b), forward through the 1 A bead in R1 and up through the 1 B and 1 C beads just added in this step.

d) Repeat (b, c) around 4 more times.
Pick up 8A, go with thread down through the 2nd C bead and the 2nd B bead added at (a) and right to left through the 1 A bead in R1.

e) Continue with working thread up through the 1st B bead, the 1st C bead and the 1 E bead added at (a).

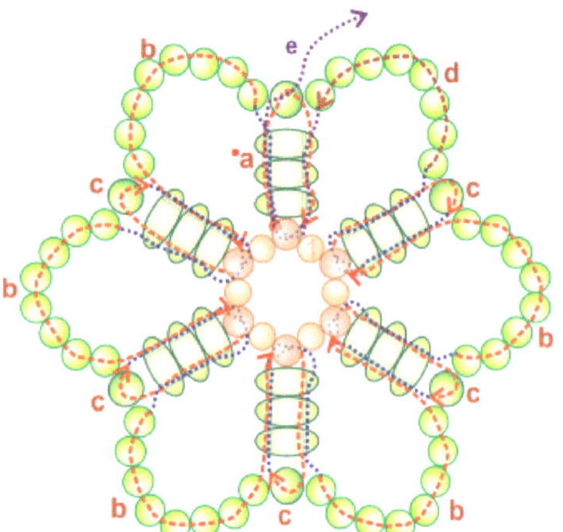

Round 2 - V1

Round 2 - V2

a) Pick up 3W, 1E, go with thread down through the opposite holes in the W beads just added, right to left through the 1 A bead in R1, and up through the left side holes of the W beads just added.

b) Pick up 8A, 3W, go with thread right to left through 1A bead in R1 as shown and up through the left side holes of the W beads just added.

c) Pick up 1E, go with thread down through the right side hole of the W beads added at (b), right to left through the 1 A bead in R1, and up through the left side hole of the W beads added at (b).

d) Repeat (b, c) around 4 more times.
Pick up 8A, go with thread down through the right side hole of the W beads added at (a) and right to left through the 1 A bead in R1.

e) Continue with working thread up through the left side holes in the W beads and left to right through the 1 E bead added at (a).

Round 2 - V2

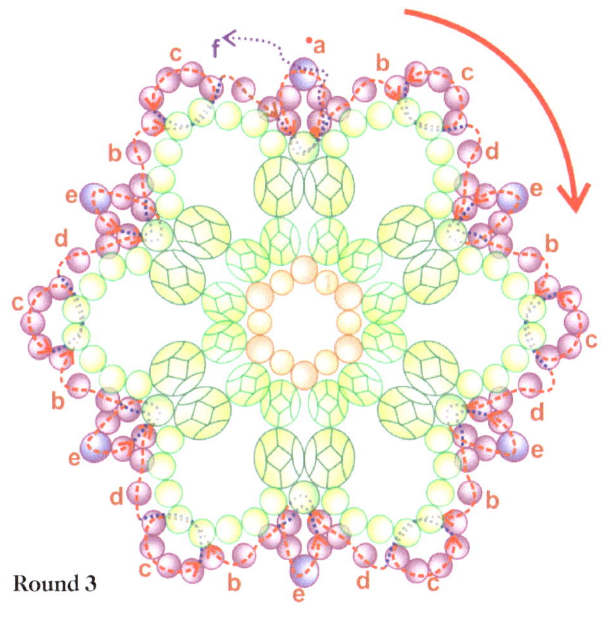

Round 3

Round 3 - V1 and V2
This Round is worked Clockwise

a) Pick up 2A, 1E, 2A, go with thread left to right through the 1 E bead, R2a or R2c, and up through the 1st A bead just added.

b) Pick up 3A, go with thread left to right through the 5th and 4th A beads, R2b or R2d.

c) Pick up 4A, go with thread forward through the 3rd A bead added at (b), left to right through the 5th and 4th A beads, R2b or R2d, and forward through the 1st A bead just added.

d) Pick up 3A, go with thread left to right through the 1 E bead, R2a or R2c.

e) Pick up 2A, 1E, 1A, go with thread forward through the 3rd A bead added at (d), right to left through the 1 E bead, R2a or R2c, and up through the 1st A bead just added.

f) Repeat (b, c, d, e) around 4 more times. Repeat (b,c) 1 time. Pick up 2A, go with thread down through the last A bead added at (a).

g) Continue with working thread left to right through the E bead, R2a, up and then right to left through the 1st 2 A beads and E bead added at (a).

Round 4 - V1
This Round is worked Counter - Clockwise

a) Pick up 3A, go with thread right to left through the E bead and the down through the 3rd A bead, R3a or R3e.

b) Pick up 4A, go with thread right to left through the 2nd and 3rd A beads, R3c.

c) Pick up 4A, 1B, 2A, 1B, 4A, go with thread right to left through the 3rd A bead, R3c, and up through the first 4 A beads and the 1st B bead added at (c).

d) Pick up 1C, 2A, 1C, go with thread down through the 2nd B bead and the second set of 4 A beads added at (c), right to left through the 3rd and 4th A beads, R3c.

e) Pick up 4A, go with thread up and then right to left through the A bead and E bead, R3a or R3e.

f) Repeat (a, b, c, d, e) around 5 more times.

g) Continue with working thread forward through the 1st and 2nd A beads added in this Round at the first repeat of (a).

Round 4 - V2
This Round is worked Counter - Clockwise

a) Pick up 3A, go with thread right to left through the E bead and the down through the 3rd A bead, R3a or R3e.

b) Pick up 4A, go with thread right to left through the 2nd and 3rd A beads, R3c.

c) Pick up 4A, 1W, 2A, 1W, 4A, go with thread right to left through the 3rd A bead, R3c, and up through the first 4 A beads and the 1st W bead added at (c).

d) Pick up 2W, 2A, 2W, go with thread down through the left hole in the 2nd W bead and the second set of 4 A beads added at (c), right to left through the 3rd and 4th A beads, R3c.

e) Pick up 4A, go with thread up and then right to left through the A bead and E bead, R3a or R3e.

f) Repeat (a, b, c, d, e) around 5 more times.

g) Continue with working thread forward through the 1st and 2nd A beads added in this Round at the first repeat of (a).

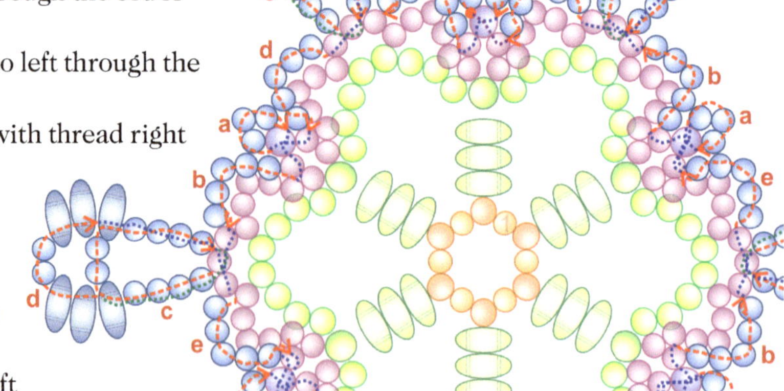

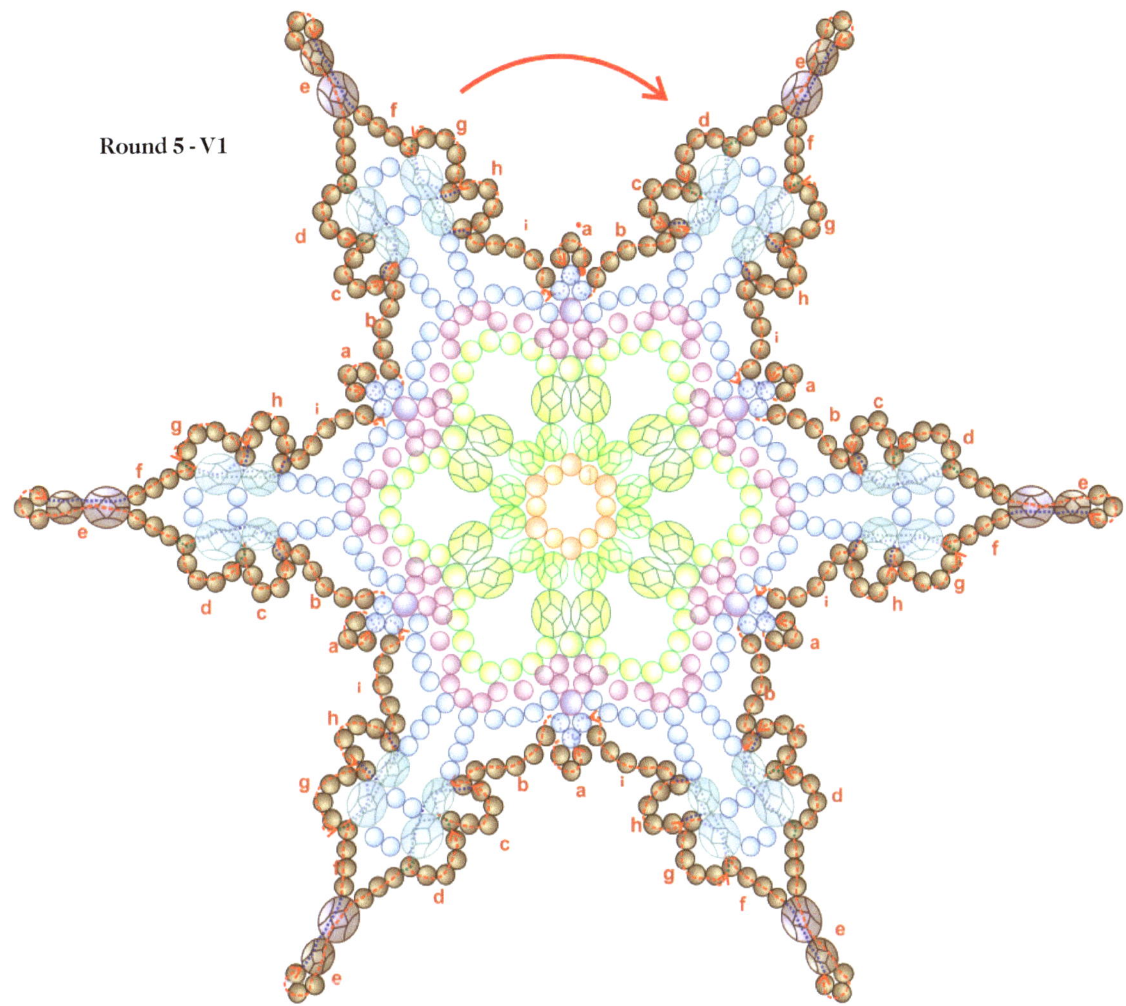

Round 5 - V1

a) Pick up 3A, go with thread left to right 2nd and 3rd A beads, R4a.

b) Pick up 6A, go with thread up through the 1st B bead, R4c.

c) Pick up 5A, go with thread up through the 6th A bead added at (b) and the 1st B bead, R4c and the 1st C bead, R4d.

d) Pick up 5A, go with thread forward through the 1st A bead added at (c), the C bead, R4d and the 1st A bead just added in this step.

e) Pick up 3A, 1C, 1B, 3A, go with thread down through the 1 B and the 1 C beads just added.

f) Pick up 4A, go with thread down through the 2nd C bead, R4d.

g) Pick up 5A, go with thread forward through the 4th A bead added at (f), the C bead, R4d and the B bead, R4c.

h) Pick up 5A, go with thread forward through the 1st A bead added at (g), the B bead, R4c and the 1st A bead just added in this step.

i) Pick up 5A, go with thread left to right through the 1st and 2nd A beads, R4a.

j) Repeat (a, b, c, d, e, f, g, h, i) around 5 more times.

k) Weave the working thread into the snowflake and end.

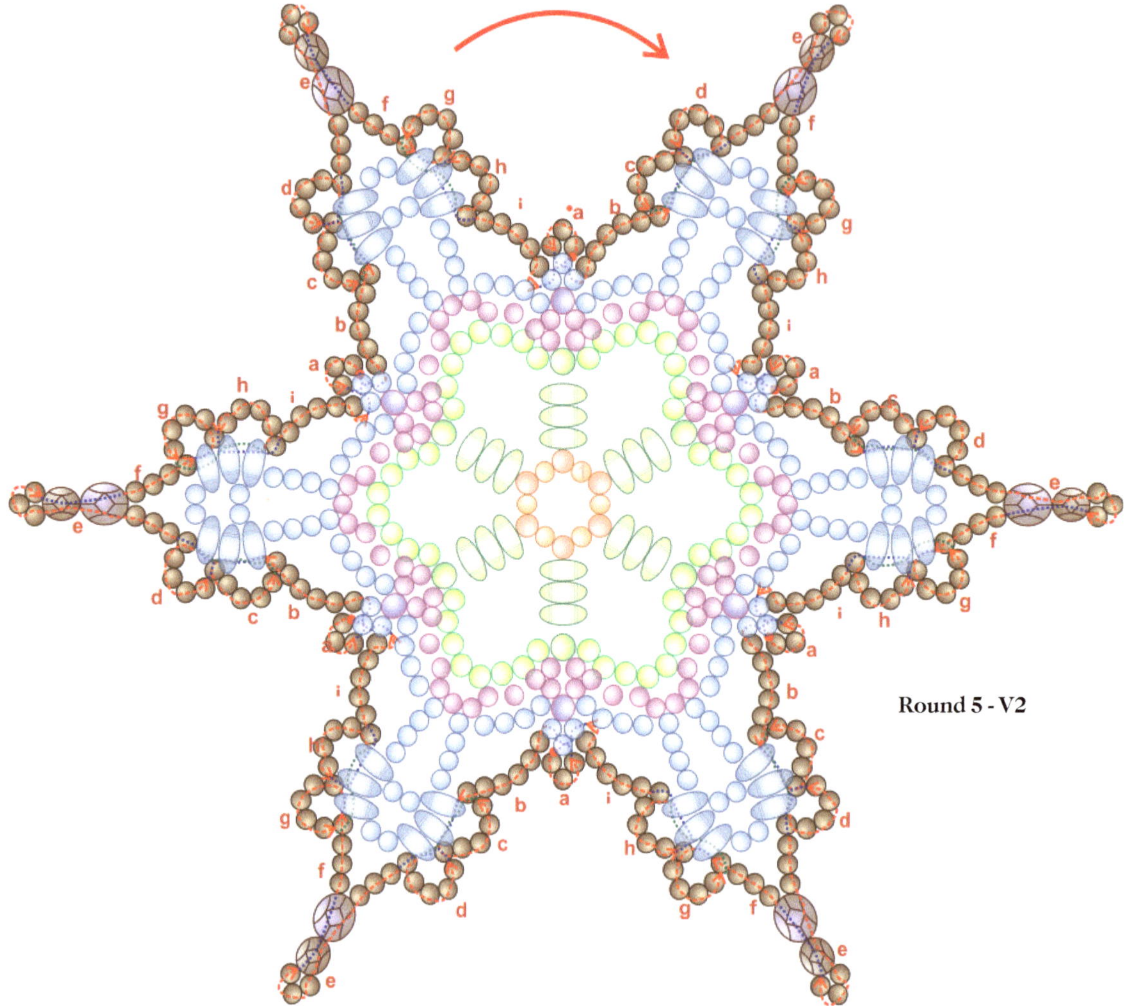

Round 5 - V2

a) Pick up 3A, go with thread left to right 2nd and 3rd A beads, R4a.

b) Pick up 6A, go with thread up through the left side hole in the W bead, R4c and the left side hole in the 1st W bead, R4d.

c) Pick up 5A, go with thread up through the 6th A bead added at (b), left side hole in the W bead, R4c and left side hole in the 2 W beads, R4d.

d) Pick up 5A, go with thread forward through the 5th A bead added at (c), the left side hole of the 2nd W bead, R4d and the 1st A bead just added in this step.

e) Pick up 3A, 1C, 1B, 3A, go with thread down through the 1 B and the 1 C beads just added.

f) Pick up 4A, go with thread down through the right side hole of the 3rd W bead, R4d.

g) Pick up 5A, go with thread forward through the 4th A bead added at (f), the right side holes of the 3rd and 4th W beads, R4d and the right side hole of the 2nd W bead, R4c.

h) Pick up 5A, go with thread forward through the 5th A bead added at (g), the right side hole of the 4th W bead, R4d, the right side hole in the 2nd W bead, R4c and the 1st A bead just added.

i) Pick up 5A, go with thread left to right through the 1st and 2nd A beads, R4a.

j) Repeat (a, b, c, d, e, f, g, h, i) around 5 more times.

k) Weave the working thread into the snowflake and end.

Gleam Snowflake Ornament

3-1/4 Inches

Version 1

A = Miyuki 11° SEED bead,
   780 beads
C = 4 mm Fire-polished crystals,
   6 crystals
E = Miyuki 8° SEED bead,
   12 beads

Version 2

A = Miyuki 11° SEED bead,
   780 beads
T = Tila Beads,
   18 beads
E = Miyuki 8° SEED bead,
   12 beads

Round 1 - V1 and V2

Pick up 6E, go with thread forward through the 1st E bead. Continue with thread around through all 6 E beads again coming out with thread at the 1st E bead.

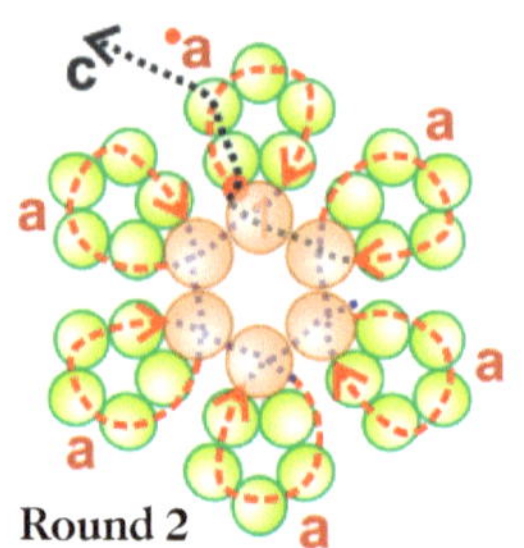
Round 2

Round 2 - V1 and V2

a) Pick up 5A, go with thread forward through the same bead that your working thread is exiting and continue forward through the next E bead in R1 as shown.

b) Repeat (a) around 5 more times.

c) Continue with working thread forward through the 1st and 2nd A beads added in the first repeat of (a) this Round.

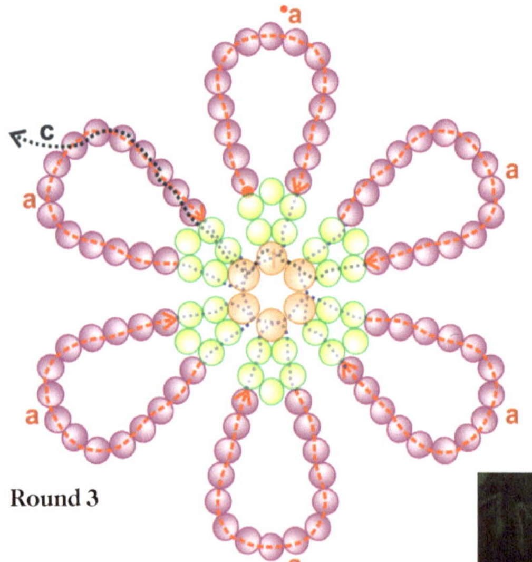
Round 3

Round 3 - V1 and V2

a) Pick up 15A, go with thread down through the 4th and 5th A Beads, R2, forward through 2 E beads, R1, and up through the 1st and 2nd A beads R2.

b) Repeat (a) around 5 more times.

c) Continue after completing the last repeat of (a), go with working thread through 3 E beads, and up through the 15th through 9th A beads this round added at the first repeat of (a).

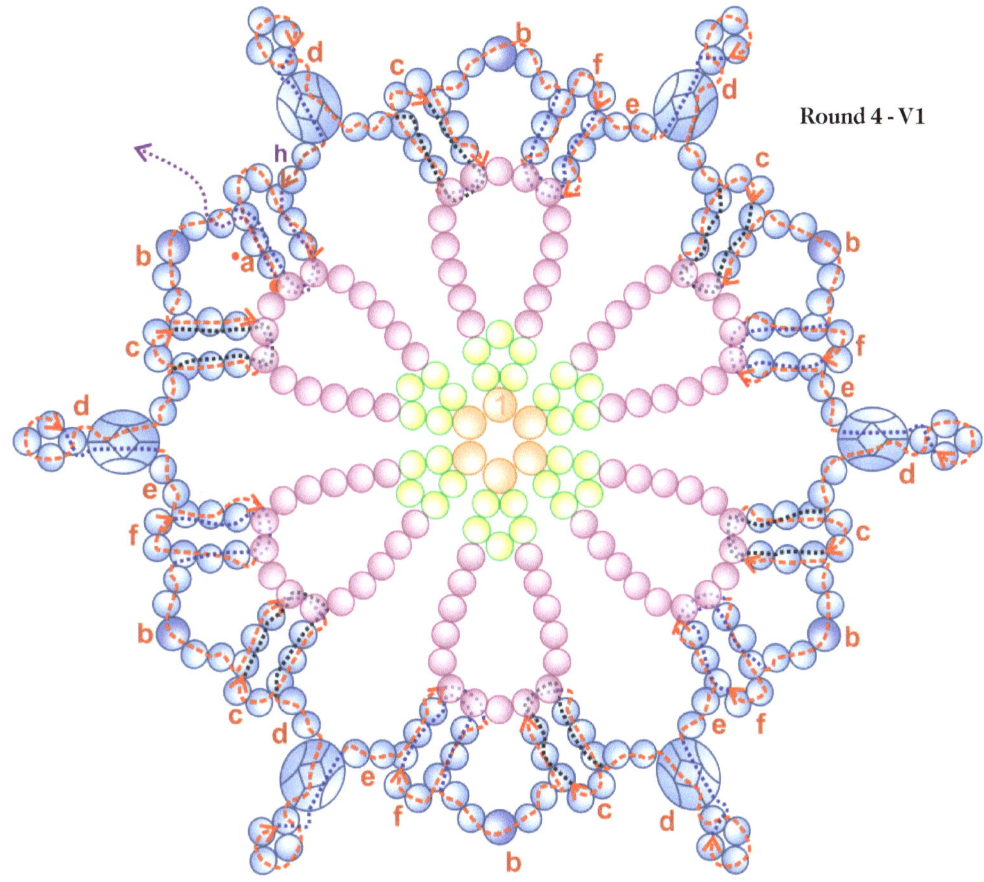

Round 4 - V1

a) Pick up 8A, go with thread right to left through the 10th and 9th A beads, R3a and up through the 1st, 2nd and 3rd A beads just added.

b) Pick up 2A, 1E, 5A, go with thread right to left through the 7th and 6th A beads, R3a.

c) Pick up 5A, go with thread down through the 3rd, 4th and 5th A beads added at (b) and right to left through the 7th and 6th A beads, R3a and up through the 1st, 2nd and 3rd A beads just added in this step.

d) Pick up 2A, 1C, 4A, go with thread down through the 4th A bead (of the 4A), and the C bead just added in this step.

e) Pick up 5A, go with thread right to left through the 10th and 9th A beads, R3a.

f) Pick up 5A, go with thread down through the 3rd, 4th and 5th A beads added in the last step, right to left through the 10th and 9th A beads, R3a and up through the 1st, 2nd and 3rd A beads just added in this step..

g) Repeat (b, c, d, e, f) around 4 more times.
Repeat (b, c, d) 1 time.

h) Pick up 2A, go with thread down through the 6th, 7th and 8th A beads added in this Round at (a), right to left through the 10th and 9th A beads, R3a, up through the 1st, 2nd and 3rd A beads added at (a), and right to left through the 1st A bead added at (b).

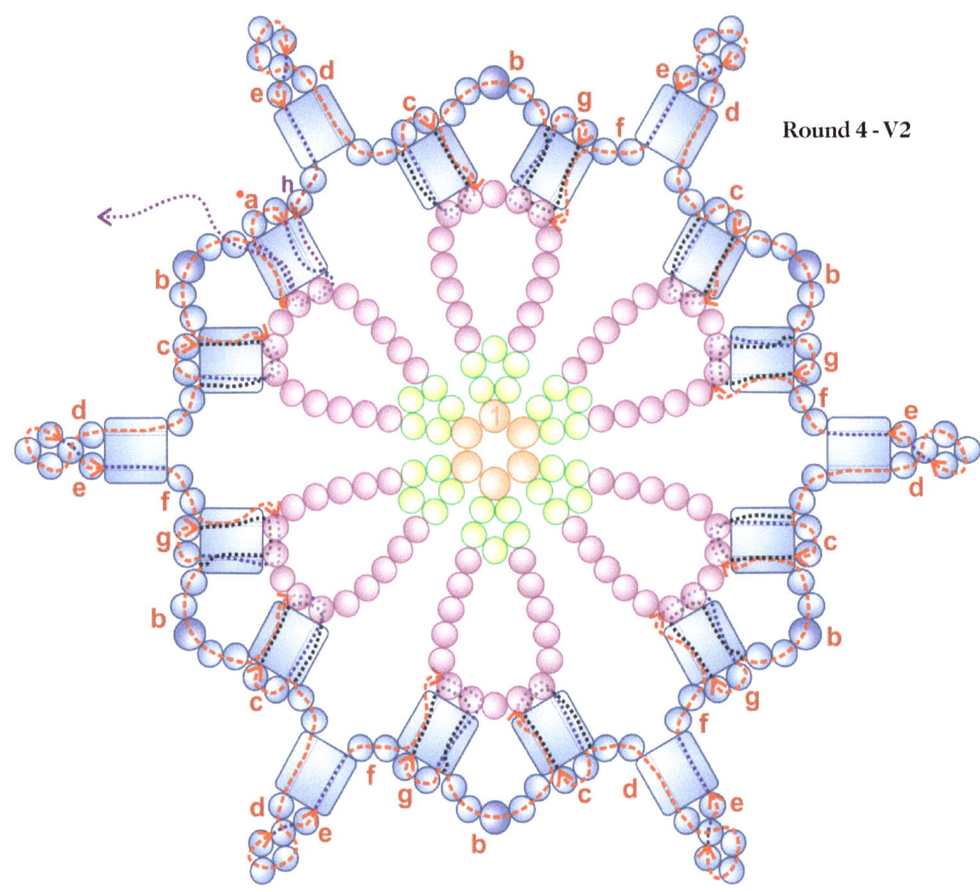

Round 4 - V2

a) Pick up 1T, 2A, go with thread down through the right side hole of the T bead, right to left through the 10th and 9th A beads, R3a, and up through the left side hole of the T bead.

b) Pick up 2A, 1E, 2A, 1T, go with thread right to left through the 7th and 6th A beads, R3a and up through the left side hole of the T bead just added.

c) Pick up 2A, go with thread down through the right side hole of the T bead added at (b), right to left through the 7th and 6th A beads, R3a and up through the left side hole of the T bead added at (b).

d) Pick up 2A*, 1T, 5A, go with thread forward through the 2nd A bead (of the 5A) just added. *In the illustration this step shows picking up 2 A beads but it works better only picking up 1 A bead.

e) Pick up 1A, go with thread down through the left side hole of the T bead added at (d).

f) Pick up 2A*, 1T, go with thread right to left through the 10th and 9th A beads, R3a and up through the left side hole of the T bead just added. *In the illustration this step shows picking up 2 A beads but it works better only picking up 1 A bead.

g) Pick up 2A, go with thread down through the right side hole of the T bead added at (f), right to left through the 10th and 9th A beads, R3a, and up through the left side hole of the T bead.

h) Repeat (b, c, d, e, f, g) around 4 more times.

Repeat (b, c, d, e) 1 time.

i) Pick up 2A, go with thread down through the right side hole of the T bead added in this Round at (a), right to left through the 10th and 9th A beads, R3a, up through the left side hole of the T bead added at (a), and right to left through the 1st A bead added at (b).

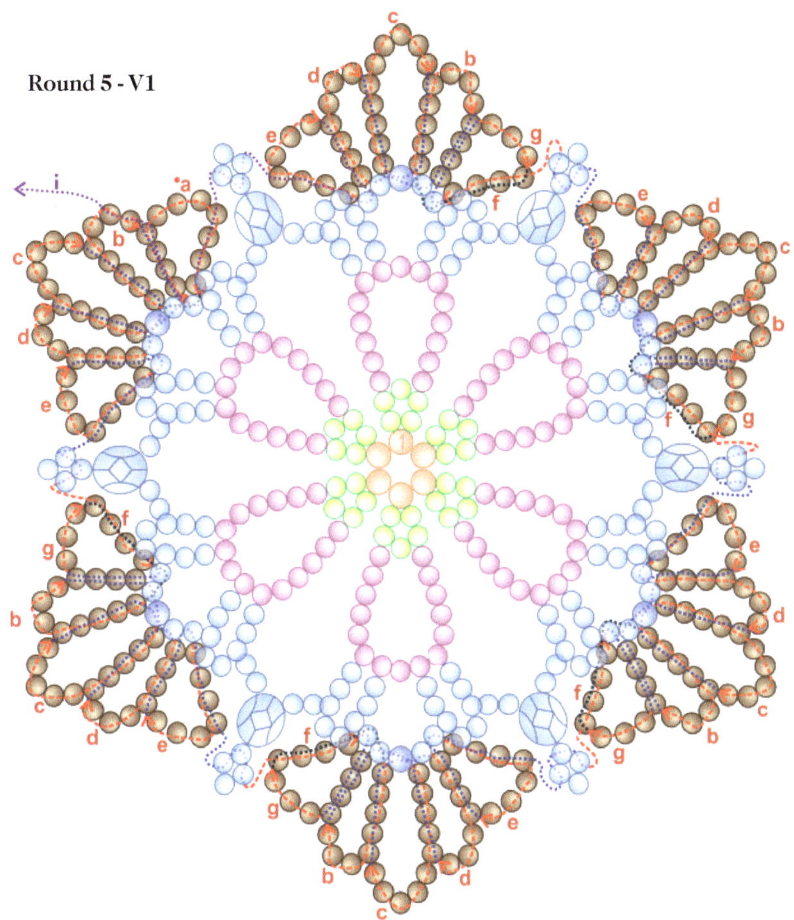

Round 5 - V1 and V2

a) Pick up 11A, go with thread right to left through the 1st and 2nd A beads, R4b.

b) Pick up 8A, go with thread down through the 4th, 3rd, 2nd and 1st A beads added at (a) or (g), right to left through the 2nd A and 1 E beads, R4b.

c) Pick up 10A, go with thread down through the 5th, 4th, 3rd, 2nd and 1st A beads added at (b), right to left through the 1 E and the next 1 A beads, R4b.

d) Pick up 7A, go with thread down through the 5th, 4th, 3rd, 2nd and 1st A beads added at (c), right to left through the 1st and 2nd A beads (of the 5A), R4b -V1 or the 1st and 2nd A beads (of the 2nd set of A beads), R4b-V2.

e) Pick up 7A, go with thread down through the 4th, 3rd, 2nd and 1st A beads added at (d), right to left through the 2nd A bead (of the 5A), R4b -V1 or the 2nd A bead (of the 2nd set of A beads), R4b-V2, and up through the 1st, 2nd, 3rd and 4th A beads added in this step.

V1 Continue with working thread down through the 4th A bead, right to left through the 1st A bead and then up through the 2nd A bead, R4d.

V2 Continue with working thread right to left through the 1st and 2nd A beads (of the 5A), R4d and the 1 A bead, R4e.

f) Pick up 4A, go with thread right to left through the 1st A bead, R4b.

g) Pick up 7A, go with thread down through the 4 A beads just added in the last step, right to left through the 1st and 2nd A beads, R4b.

h) Repeat (b, c, d, e, f, g) around 4 more times. Repeat (b, c, d, e) 1 time.

i) Continue with working thread through the beads shown in the illustration. Coming out with thread right to left through the 8th and 7th A beads added at (b).

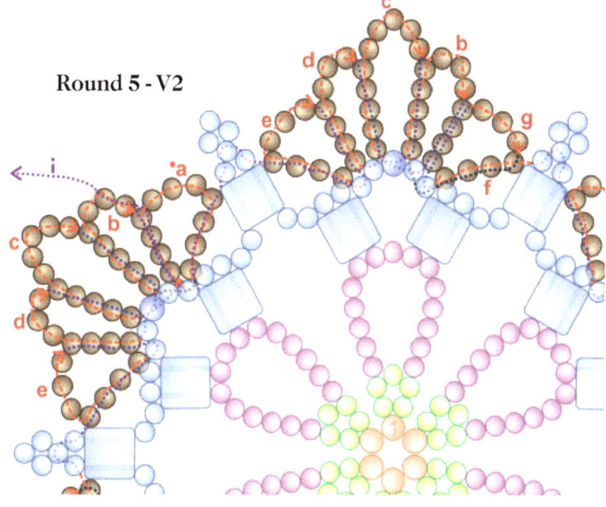

Round 6 - V1 and V2

a) Pick up 3A, go with thread right to left through the 7th and 6th A beads, R5b, and the 10th, 9th and 8th A beads, R5c.

b) Pick up 5A, go with thread right to left through the 8th A bead, R5c and forward through the 1st and 2nd A beads just added.

c) Pick up 5A, go with thread down through the 4th and 5th A beads added at (b), right to left through the 8th A bead, R5c, and up through the 1st and 2nd A beads added at (b).

d) Pick up 3A, go with thread forward through the 2nd and 3rd A beads added at (c).

e) Pick up 3A, go with thread forward through the 3rd and 4th A beads added at (c).

f) Pick up 3A, go with thread down through the 4th and 5th A beads, added at (b), right to left through the 8th, 7th and 6th A beads, R5c, and the 7th and 6th A beads, R5d.

g) Pick up 3A, go with thread right to left through the 6th and 5th A beads, R5d and the 7th and 6th A beads, R5e.

h) Pick up 3A, go with thread right to left through the 6th and 5th A beads, R5e.

i) Pick up 3A (V1) or 2A (V2), go with thread right to left through the 3rd A bead, R4d -V1 or the 4th A bead, R4d-V2.

j) Pick up 3A, go with thread right to left through the 3rd A bead, R4d -V1 or the 4th A bead, R4d-V2.

k) Pick up 3A (V1) or 2A (V2), go with thread right to left through the 7th and 6th A beads, R5a or R5g.

l) Pick up 3A, go with thread right to left through the 6th and 5th A beads, R5a or R5g and 8th and 7th A beads, R5b.

n) Repeat (a, b, c, d, e, f, g, h, i, j, k, l) around 5 more times.

o) Weave the working thread into the snowflake and end.

Twinkle Snowflake Ornament
3 Inches

1 Version
A = Miyuki 11° SEED bead,
    750 beads,
      I used a random combination of color beads

Round 1

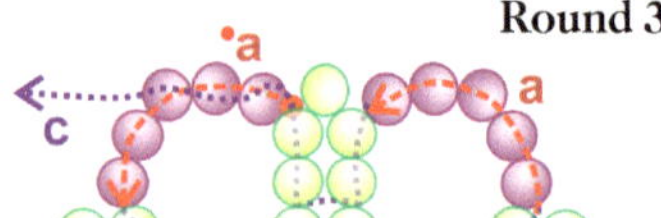

Pick up 6A, go with thread forward through the 1st A bead. Continue with thread around through all 6 A beads again coming out with thread at the 1st A bead.

Round 2

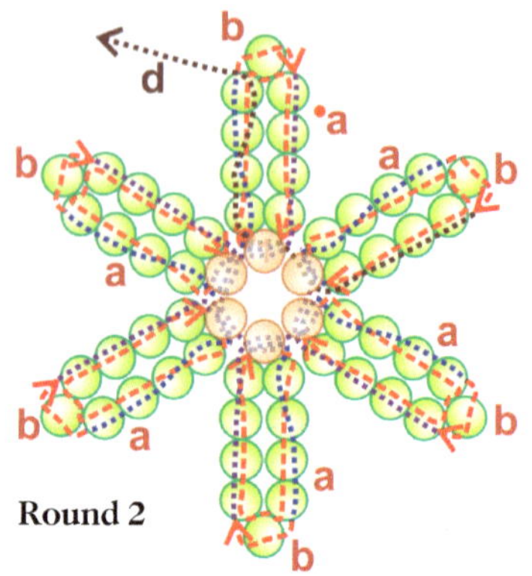

Round 2

a) Pick up 8A, go with thread right to left through 1 A bead in R1 and up through the 1st, 2nd, 3rd and 4th A beads just added.
b) Pick up 1A, go with thread down through the 5th, 6th, 7th and 8th A beads added at (a) and right to left through 2 A beads in R1 as shown.
c) Repeat (a, b) around 5 more times.
d) Continue with working thread up through the 1st, 2nd, 3rd and 4th A beads added at the first repeat of (a) in this Round.

Round 3

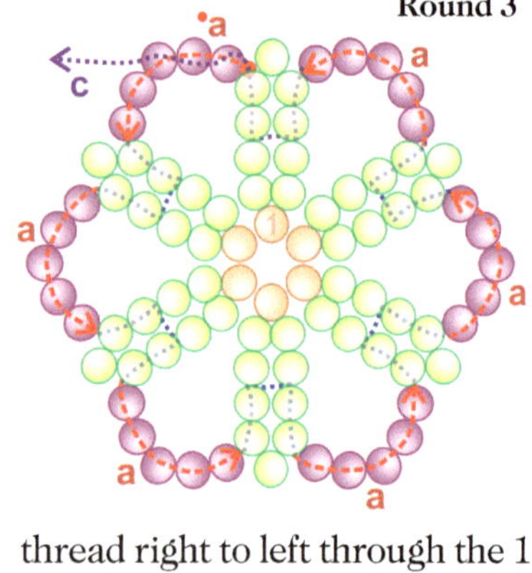

Round 3

Round 3

a) Pick up 5A, go with thread down through the 5th and 6th A beads and up through the 3rd and 4th A beads, R2a.
b) Repeat (a) around 5 more times.
c) Continue with working thread forward though the 1st, 2nd and 3rd A beads added at the first repeat of (a) in this Round.

Round 4

a) Pick up 5A, go with thread right to left through the 1 A bead, R2b.
b) Pick up 2A, go with thread right to left through the 5th A bead added at (a) or the 4th A bead this Round at (e), the 1 A bead, R2b and the 1st A bead just added in this step.
c) Pick up 4A, go with thread right to left through the 3rd A bead, R3a.
d) Pick up 4A, go with thread right to left through the 4th A bead added at (c), the 3rd A bead, R3a and the 1st A bead just added in this step.
e) Pick up 4A, go with thread right to left through the 1 A bead, R2b.
f) Repeat (b, c, d, e) around 4 more times.
Repeat (b, c) one time. At the last repeat of (c) go with working thread forward through the 1st A bead added at (a).
g) Pick up 3A, go with thread right to left (down) through the 4th A bead added at the last repeat of (c) in this Round. Continue with working thread by following the thread path in illustration, coming out with thread right to left through the 4th A bead added at (e) and the 2nd A bead, added in this Round at the last repeat of (b), as shown.

Round 4

Round 4

Round 5

a) Pick up 11A, go with thread right to left through the 2nd A bead, R4b and up through the 1st through 5th A beads just added.

b) Pick up 5A, go with thread up through the 5th A bead added at (a).

c) Pick up 8A, go with thread forward through the 3rd A bead just added.

d) Pick up 8A, go with thread forward through the 3rd A bead just added.

e) Pick up 7A, go with thread forward through the 2nd A bead just added.

f) Pick up 8A, go with thread forward through the 3rd A bead just added.

g) Pick up 2A, go with thread down through the 7th A bead added at (a).

h) Pick up 5A, go with thread down through the 7th though 11th A beads added at (a), right to left through the 2nd A bead, R4b and the 1st and 2nd A beads, R4e.

i) Pick up 2A, go with thread left to right through the 3rd A bead, R4d or R4g.

j) Pick up 4A, go with thread left to right through the 2nd A bead added at (i), the 3rd A bead, R4d or R4g and the 1st A bead just added in this step.

k) Pick up 1A, go with thread right to left through the 3rd and 4th A beads, R4a or the 2nd and 3rd A beads R4e, and the 2nd A bead, R4b.

l) Repeat (a, b, c, d, e, f, g, h, i, j, k) around 5 more times.

m) Continue with working thread through Round 4 and Round 5 as shown in the illustration coming out with thread right to left through the 4th and 3rd A beads added in this Round at the first repeat of (j).

Round 6

a) Pick up 3A, go with thread up through the 3rd A bead, R5h.

b) Pick up 1A, go with thread up through the 3rd A bead, R5h.

c) Pick up 2A, go with thread up through the 6th A bead, R5f.

d) Pick up 1A, go with thread up through the 6th A bead, R5f.

e) Pick up 2A, go with thread up through the 5th A bead, R5e.

f) Pick up 1A, go with thread up through the 5th A bead, R5e.

g) Pick up 8A, go with thread forward through the 5th A bead just added.

h) Pick up 4A, go with thread down through the 6th A bead, R5d.

i) Pick up 1A, go with thread down through the 6th A bead, R5d.

j) Pick up 2A, go with thread down through the 6th A bead, R5c.

k) Pick up 1A, go with thread down through the 6th A bead, R5c.

l) Pick up 2A, go with thread down through the 3rd A bead, R5b.

m) Pick up 1A, go with thread down through the 3rd A bead, R5b.

n) Pick up 3A, go with thread right to left through the 3rd A bead, R5j.

o) Repeat (a, b, c, d, e, f, g, h, i, j, k, l, m, n) around 5 more times.

p) Weave the working thread into the snowflake and end.

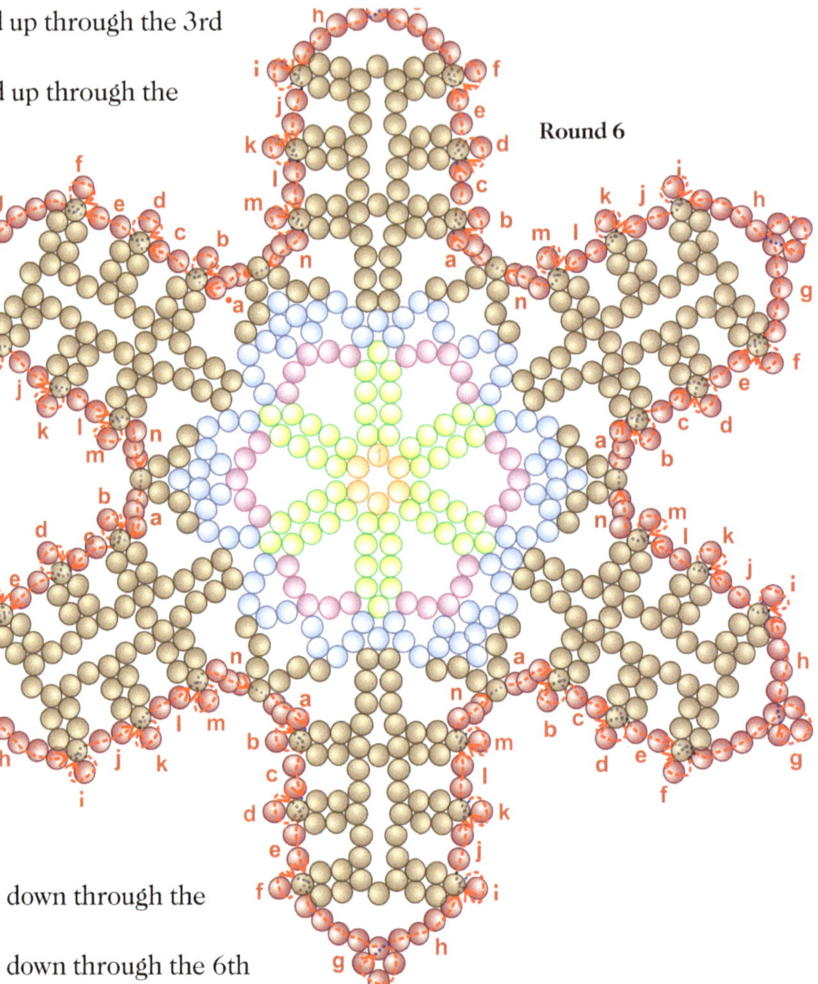

Glimmer Snowflake Ornament

2-1/4 Inches

Version 1

A = Miyuki 11° SEED bead,
     320 beads
B = 3 mm Fire-polished crystals,
     36 crystals
C = 4 mm Fire-polished crystals,
     24 crystals

Version 2

A = Miyuki 11° SEED bead,
     320 beads
B = 3 mm Fire-polished crystals,
     36 crystals
T = Tila Beads,
     12 beads

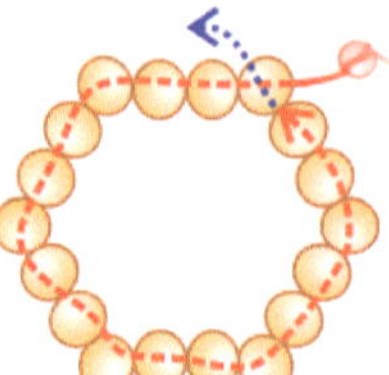

Round 1 - V1 and V2

Pick up 18A, go with thread forward through the 1st A bead. Continue with thread around through all 18 A beads again coming out with thread at the 1st A bead.

Round 2 - V1 and V2

a) Pick up 3A, skip over 2 A beads and go with thread forward through the A bead in R1 as shown.
b) Repeat (a) around 5 more times.
c) Continue with working thread forward through the 1st and 2nd A beads added in the first repeat of (a) this Round.

Round 3 - V1 and V2

a) Pick up 8A, go with thread right to left through the 2nd A bead, R2a, and up through the 1st A bead just added in this step.
b) Pick up 7A, go with thread right to left through the 2nd A bead, R2a.
c) Pick up 7A, go with thread down through the 7th A bead added in this round at (b), right to left through the 2nd A bead, R2a, and up through the 1st A bead just added in this step.
d) Repeat (b, c) around 4 more times.
e) Pick up 6A, go with thread down through the 8th A bead added in this Round at (a), right to left through the 2nd A bead, R2a, and forward (up) through the 1st through 5th A beads added in this Round at (a).

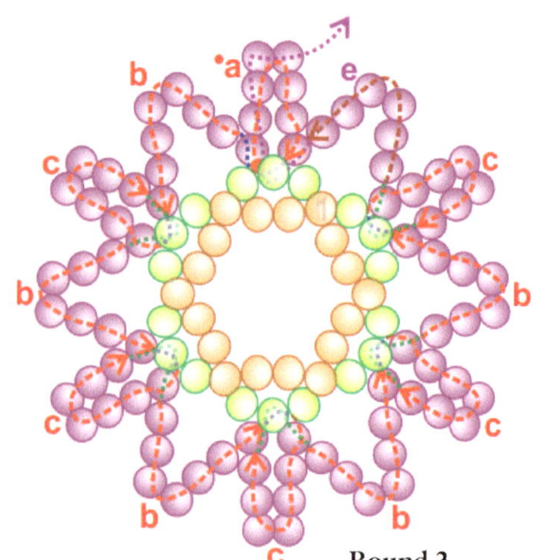

Round 2

Round 3

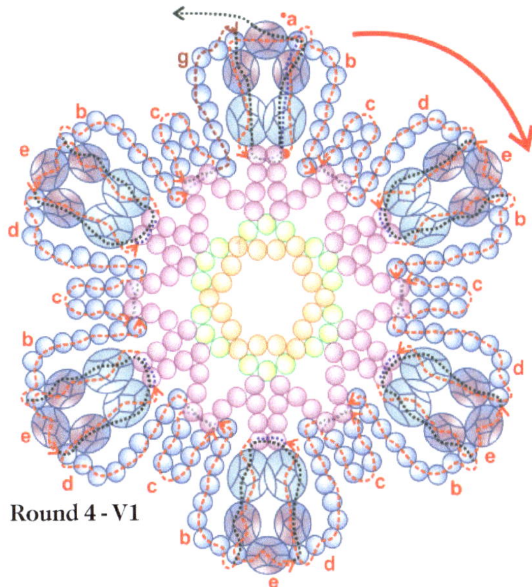

Round 4 - V1

Round 4 - V1

This Round is worked Clockwise

a) Pick up 1C, 1B, 1A, 1B, 1A, 1B, 1C, go with thread left to right through the 4th and 5th A beads, R3a or R3c, and up through 1st C bead, the 1st B bead and the 1st A bead just added in this step.

b) Pick up 8A, go with thread left to right through the 4th and 3rd A beads, R3e or R3b.

c) Pick up 6A, go with thread left to right through the 4th and 3rd A beads, R3e or R3b.

d) Pick up 9A, 1B, 1C, go with thread left to right through the 4th and 5th A beads, R3a or R3c.

e) Pick up 1C, 1B, 1A, 1B, go with thread down through 9th A, the B bead and the C bead added in this Round at (d), left to right through the 4th and 5th A beads, R3a or R3c, and up through 1st C bead, the 1st B bead and the 1st A bead just added in this step.

f) Repeat (b, c, d, e) around 4 more times. Repeat (b, c) 1 time.

g) Pick up 8A, go with thread down through the 2nd A bead, the 3rd B bead and the 2nd C bead added in this Round at (a), left to right through the 4th and 5th A beads, R3a or R3c, and up through 1st C bead, the 1st B bead, the 1st A bead and right to left through the 2nd B bead added in this Round at (a).

Round 4 - V2

This Round is worked Clockwise

a) Pick up 1T, 1B, 1A, 1B, 1A, 1B, go with thread down through the left side hole in the T bead, left to right through the 4th and 5th A beads, R3a or R3c, and up through the right side hole of the T bead, the 1st B bead and the 1st A bead just added in this step.

b) Pick up 8A, go with thread left to right through the 4th and 3rd A beads, R3e or R3b.

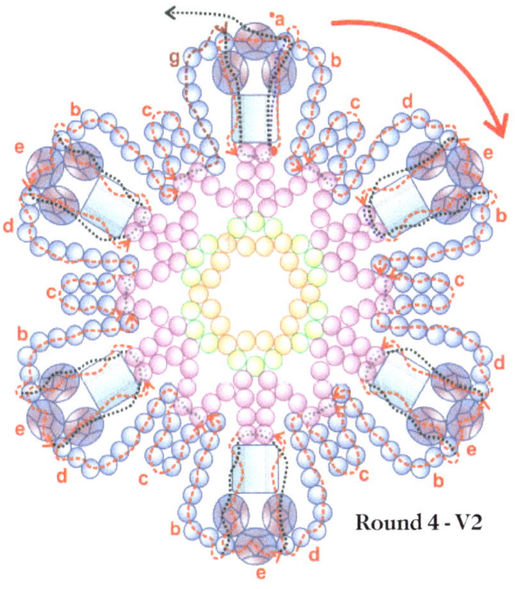

Round 4 - V2

c) Pick up 6A, go with thread left to right through the 4th and 3rd A beads, R3e or R3b.

d) Pick up 9A, 1B, 1T, go with thread left to right through the 4th and 5th A beads, R3a or R3c, and up through the right side hole of the T bead.

e) Pick up 1B, 1A, 1B, go with thread down through 9th A, the B bead and the left side hole of the T bead added in this Round at (d), left to right through the 4th and 5th A beads, R3a or R3c, and up through right side hole of the T bead, the 1st B bead and the 1st A bead just added in this step.

f) Repeat (b, c, d, e) around 4 more times. Repeat (b, c) 1 time.

g) Pick up 8A, go with thread down through the 2nd A bead, the 3rd B bead and the left side hole of the T bead added in this Round at (a), left to right through the 4th and 5th A beads, R3a or R3c, and up through right side hole of the T bead, the 1st B bead, the 1st A bead and right to left through the 2nd B bead added in this Round at (a).

Round 5 - V1
This Round is worked Counter-Clockwise

a) Pick up 5A, go with thread right to left through the 2nd B bead, R4a or R4e.

b) Pick up 2A, go with thread down through the 8th through 4th A beads, R4d or R4g, right to left through the 3rd and 4th A beads, R4c.

c) Pick up 1C, 1B, 1A, 1B, 1A, 1B, 1C, go with thread right to left through the 3rd and 4th A beads, R4c , and up through the 5th through the 1st A beads, R4b.

d) Pick up 2A, go with thread right to left through the B bead, R4a or R4e as shown.

e) Repeat (a, b, c, d) around 5 more times.

f) Continue with working thread through the 1st, 2nd and 3rd A beads added in this Round at the first repeat of (a).

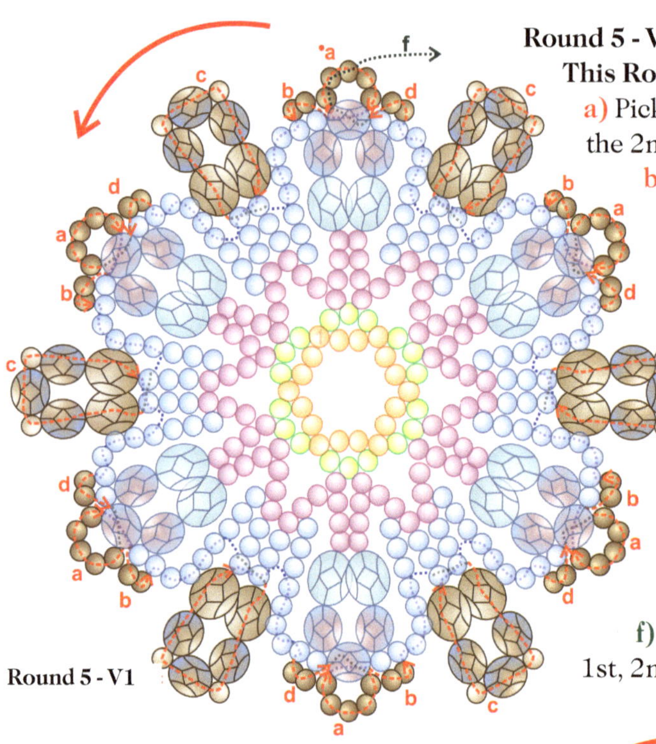

Round 5 - V1

Round 5 - V2
This Round is worked Counter-Clockwise

a) Pick up 5A, go with thread right to left through the 2nd B bead, R3a or R3e.

b) Pick up 2A, go with thread down through the 8th through 4th A beads, R4d or R4g, and right to left through the 3rd and 4th A beads, R4c.

c) Pick up 1T, 1B, 1A, 1B, 1A, 1B, go with thread down through the right side hole of the T bead just added, right to left through the 3rd and 4th A beads, R4c , up through the 5th through 1st A beads, R4b.

d) Pick up 2A, go with thread right to left through the B bead, R4a or R4e as shown.

e) Repeat (a, b, c, d) around 5 more times.

f) Continue with working thread through the 1st, 2nd and 3rd A beads added in this Round at the first repeat of (a).

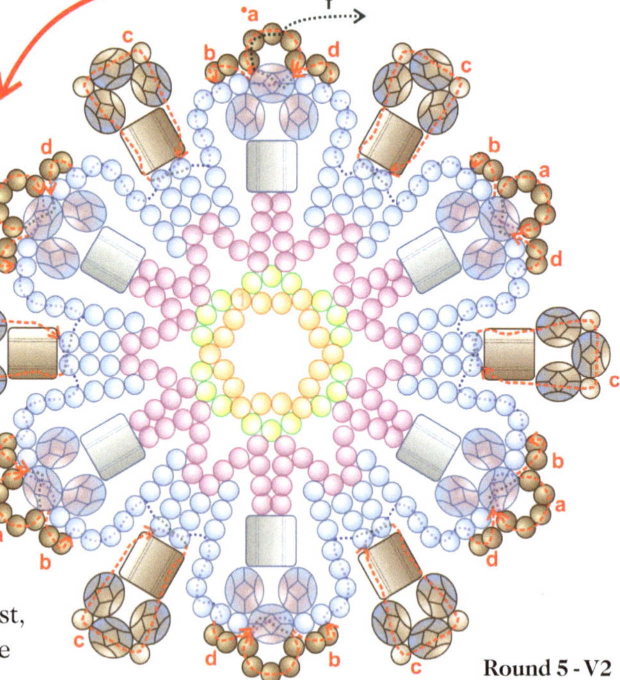

Round 5 - V2

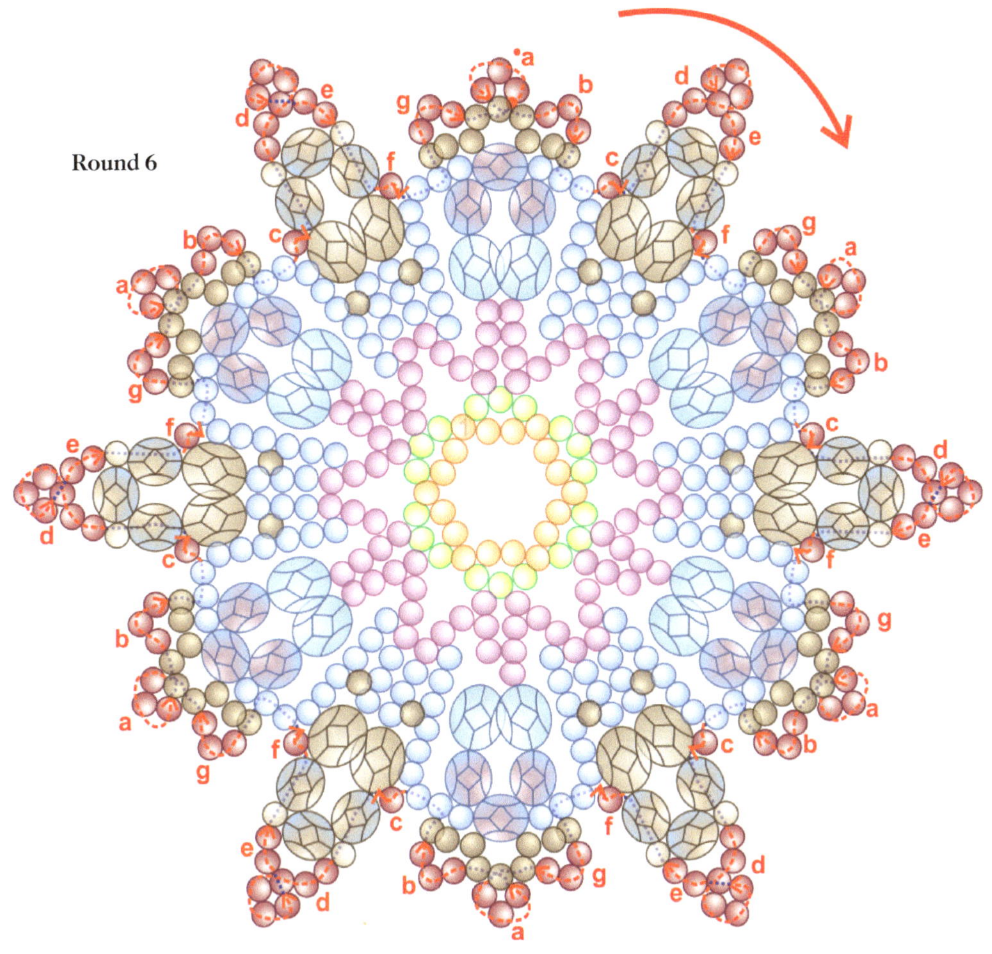

Round 6 - V1 and V2

This Round is worked Clockwise

a) Pick up 3A, go with thread left to right through the 3rd and 4th A beads, R5a.

b) Pick up 3A, go with thread left to right through the 1st A bead, R5d the 1st and 2nd A beads, R4b.

c) Pick up 1A, go with thread up through the 1 B bead and 1 A bead, 5c, as shown.

d) Pick up 6A, go with thread forward through the 3rd A bead just added.

e) Pick up 2A, go with thread down through the 2nd A bead and the 3rd B bead, R5c.

f) Pick up 1A, go with thread left to right through the 7th and 8th A beads, R4d or R4g and the 2nd A bead, R5b.

g) Pick up 3A, go with thread left to right through the 2nd and 3rd A beads, R5a.

h) Repeat (a, b, c, d, e, f, g) around 5 more times.

i) Weave the working thread into the snowflake and end.

Joyful Snowflake
Ornament

Lustrous Snowflake
Ornament

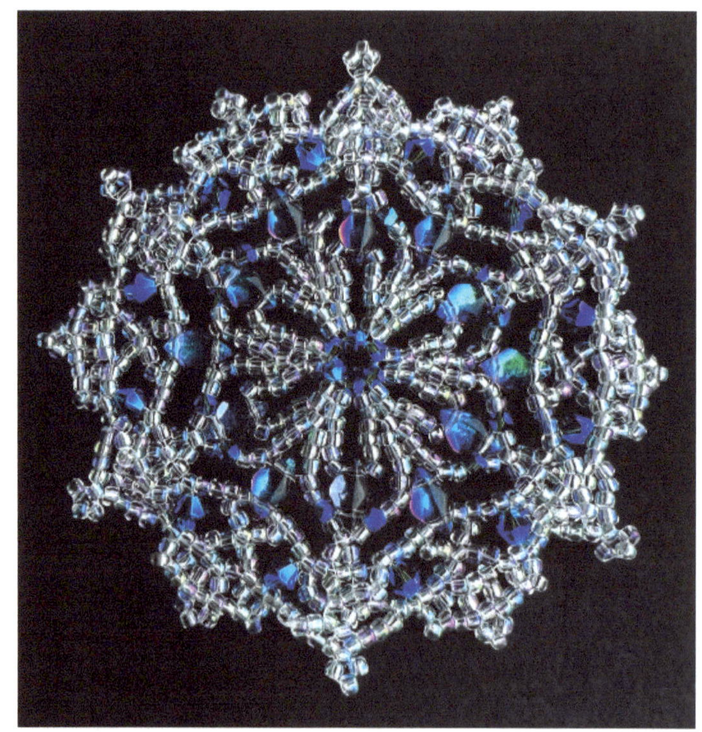

Glow Snowflake Ornament
3 Inches

One Version
A = Miyuki 11° SEED bead, main color,
     540 beads
S = Miyuki 11° SEED bead, 2nd color,
     170 beads
C = 4 mm Fire-polished crystals,
     12 crystals

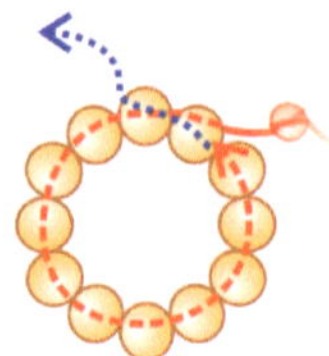

Round 1

Round 1

Pick up 12A, go with thread forward through the 1st A bead. Continue with thread around through all 12 A beads again coming out with thread at the 1st A bead.

Round 2

a) Pick up 3A, go with thread right to left through 3 A beads in R1, as shown.

b) Repeat (a) around 5 more times.

c) Continue with working thread forward through the 1st A bead added at the first repeat of (a) in this Round.

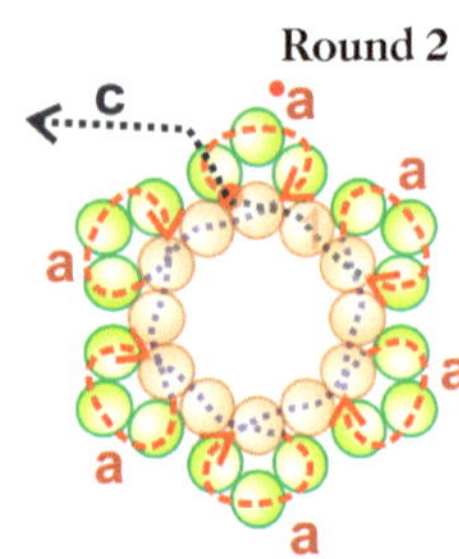

Round 3

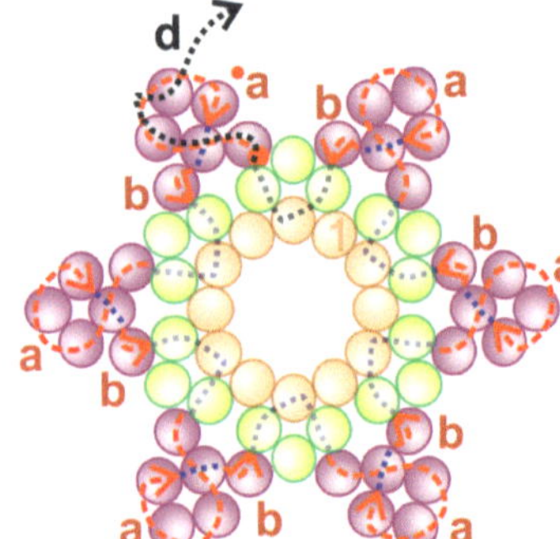

Round 3

a) Pick up 5S, go with thread forward through the 2nd S bead just added in this step.

b) Pick up 1S, go with thread down through the 3rd A bead, R2a, right to left through 1 A bead in R1, and up through the 1st A bead, R2a.

c) Repeat (a, b) around 5 more times.

d) Continue with working thread forward through the 1st, 2nd, 3rd and 4th S beads added at the first repeat of (a) in this Round.

Round 4

This Round is worked Clockwise

a) Pick up 4A, go with thread left to right through the 2nd A bead, R2a.

b) Pick up 2A, go with thread down through the 4th A bead added at the last step, left to right through the 2nd A bead, R2a, and up through the 1st A bead just added in this step.

c) Pick up 3A, go with thread left to right through the 4th S bead, R3a.

d) Repeat (a, b, c) around 5 more times. .

e) Continue with thread left to right through the 1st A bead added in the first repeat of (a) in this Round.

Round 4

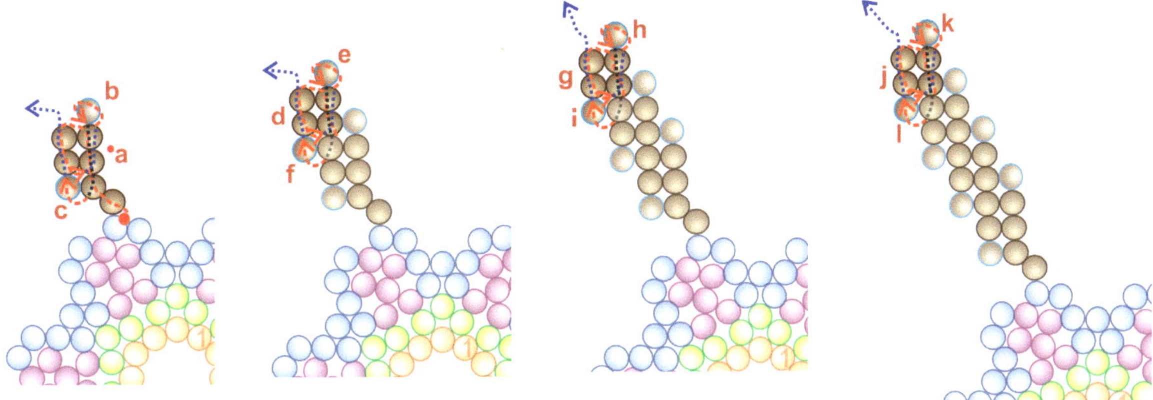

Round 5

This Round is worked Clockwise

a) Pick up 6A, go with thread up through the 3rd and 4th A beads just added.

b) Pick up 1S, go with thread down through the 4th, 3rd and 2nd A beads added at (a).

c) Pick up 1S, go with thread up through the 6th and 5th A beads added at (a).

d) Pick up 4A, go with thread up (forward) through the 1st and 2nd A beads just added.

e) Pick up 1S, go with thread down through the 2nd and 1st A beads added at (d) and the 5th A bead added at (a).

f) Pick up 1S, go with thread up through the 4th and 3rd A beads added at (d).

g) Pick up 4A, go with thread up (forward) through the 1st and 2nd A beads just added.

h) Pick up 1S, go with thread down through the 2nd and 1st A beads added at (g) and the 3rd A bead added at (d).

i) Pick up 1S, go with thread up through the 4th and 3rd A beads added at (g).

j) Pick up 4A, go with thread up (forward) through the 1st and 2nd A beads just added.

k) Pick up 1S, go with thread down through the 2nd and 1st A beads added at (j) and the 3rd A bead added at (g).

l) Pick up 1S, go with thread up through the 4th and 3rd A beads added at (j).

m) Pick up 4A, go with thread up (forward) through the 1st and 2nd A beads just added.

n) Pick up 1S, go with thread down through the 2nd and 1st A beads added at (m) and the 3rd A bead added at (j).

o) Pick up 1S, go with thread up through the 4th and 3rd A beads added at (m).

p) Pick up 3A, 1C, 3A, go with thread down through the 1 C bead and the 3rd A bead just added.

q) Pick up 6A, go with thread down (forward) through the 3rd and 4th A beads just added and the 1 S bead added at (o).

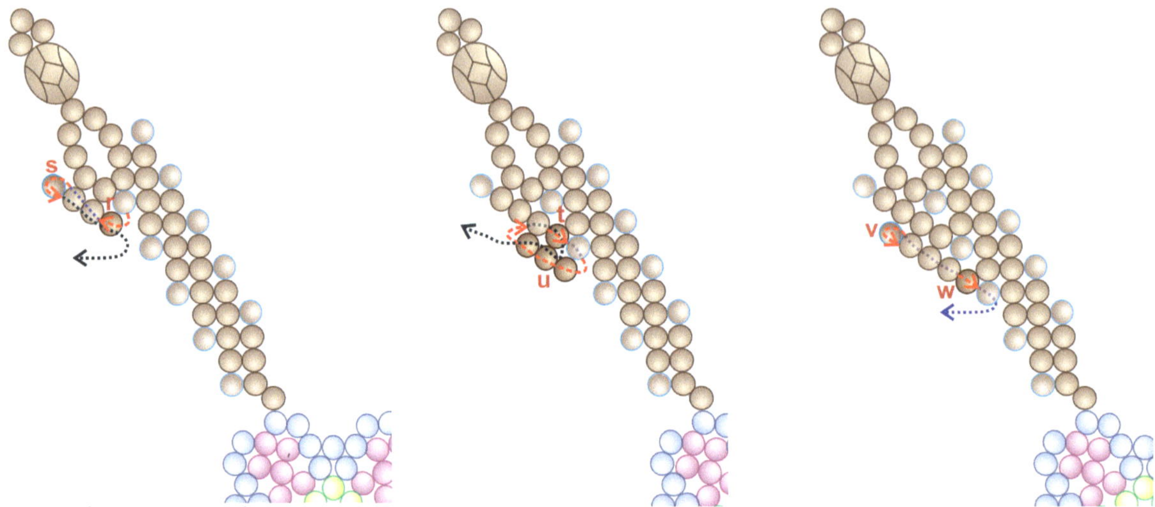

Round 5 Continued

This Round is worked Clockwise

r) Pick up 1A, go with thread up through the 5th and 6th A beads added at (q).

s) Pick up 1S, go with thread down through the 6th and 5th A beads added at (q), and the 1 A added at (r).

t) Pick up 1A, go with thread down through the 1 S bead added at (l).

u) Pick up 3A, go with thread down through the 1 A bead added at (r), the 1 A bead added at (t), and up through the 2nd and 3rd A beads just added in this step.

v) Pick up 1S, go with thread down through the 3 A beads added at (u).

w) Pick up 1A, go with thread down through the 1 S bead added at (i).

x) Pick up 3A, go with thread down through the 1st A bead added at (u), the 1 A bead added at (w), and up through the 2nd and 3rd A beads just added in this step.

y) Pick up 1S, go with thread down through the 3 A beads added at (x).

z) Pick up 1A, go with thread down through the 1 S bead added at (f).

aa) Pick up 3A, go with thread down through the 1st A bead added at (x), the 1 A bead added at (z), and up through the 2nd and 3rd A beads just added in this step.

bb) Pick up 1S, go with thread down through the 3 A beads added at (aa).

cc) Pick up 1A, go with thread down through the 1 S bead added at (c).

dd) Pick up 3A, go with thread down through the 1st A bead added at (aa), the 1 A bead added at (cc), and up through the 2nd and 3rd A beads just added in this step.

Round 5 Continued

This Round is worked Clockwise

ee) Pick up 1S, go with thread down through the 3 A beads added at (dd).

ff) Pick up 1A, go with thread left to right through the 3rd A bead, R4c, the 4th A bead, R3a and the 1st A bead, R4a.

gg) Pick up 1A, 2S, 1C, 2A, 1S, 2A, go with thread down through the C bead just added and forward (left to right) through the 2nd S bead just added.

hh) Pick up 1S, 1A, go with thread down left to right through the 3rd A bead, R4c, the 4th A bead, R3a and the 1st A bead, R4a.

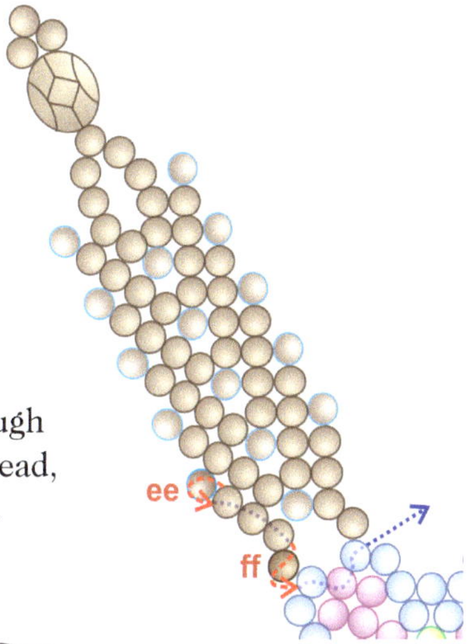

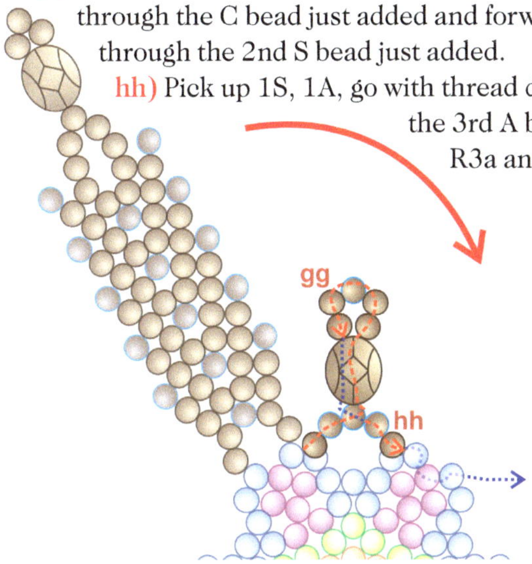

ii) Repeat (a) through (hh) around 5 more times.

jj) Continue with thread up through the beads added in (gg) as shown, coming out with thread up through the last 2 A beads added at (gg).

Round 6

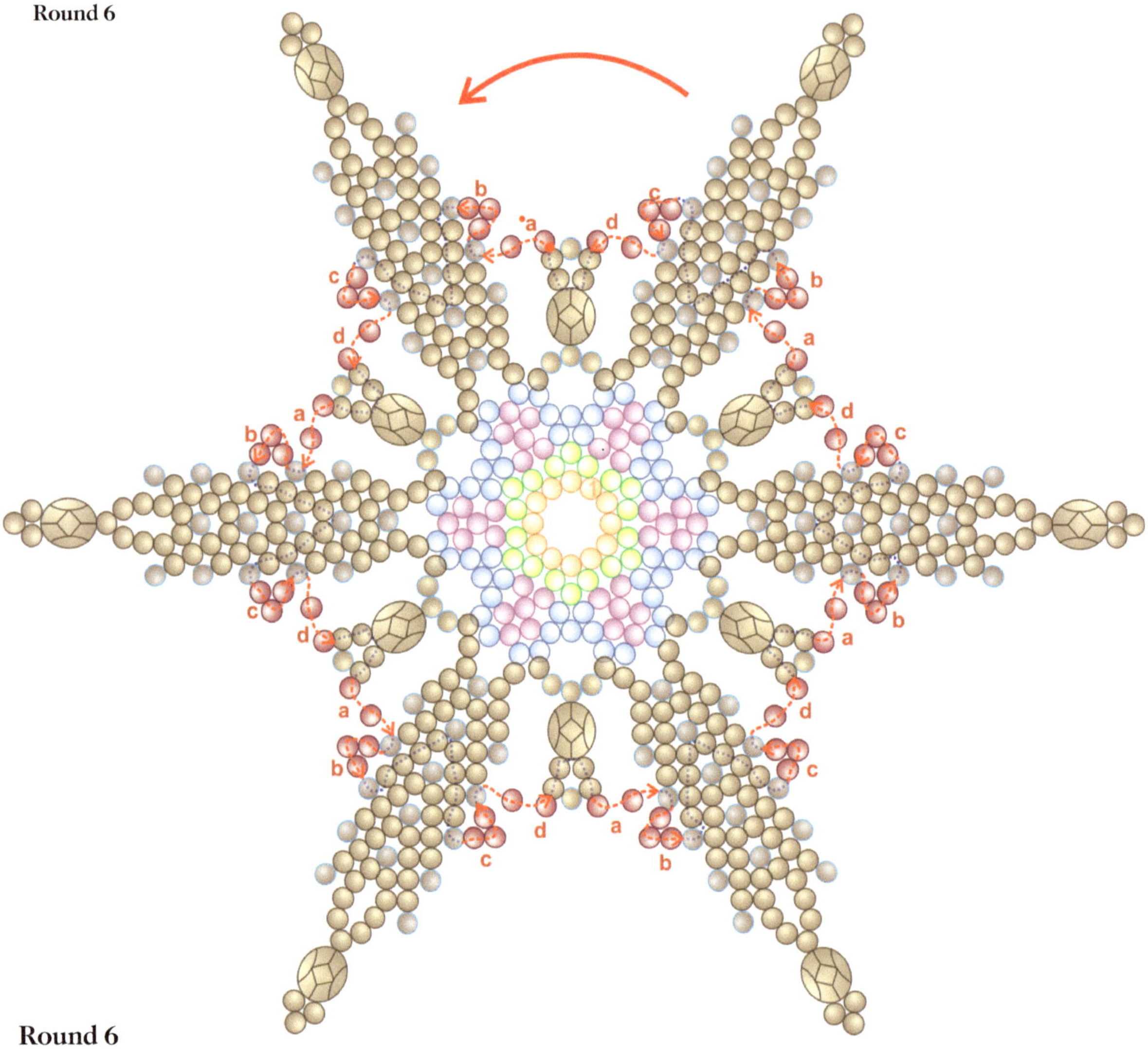

Round 6
This Round is worked Counter - Clockwise

a) Pick up 2A, go with thread up through the 1 S bead, R5e.

b) Pick up 3A, go with thread up through the 1 S bead, R5h, right to left and down angle through the 4 A beads and then up angle through 4 A beads, as shown and up thorough the 1 S bead, R5y.

c) Pick up 3A, go with thread down through the 1 S bead, R5bb.

d) Pick up 2A, go with thread down through the 2nd and 1st A beads and up through the 4th and 5th A beads, R5gg.

e) Repeat (a, b, c, d) around 5 more times.

f) Weave the working thread into the snowflake and end.

Lustrous Snowflake Ornament
2-1/2 Inches

Version 1

A = Miyuki 11° SEED bead, main color,
    360 beads

R = Miyuki 11° SEED bead, second color,
    150 beads

B = 3 mm Fire-polished crystals,
    60 crystals

Version 2

A = Miyuki 11° SEED bead, main color,
    360 beads

R = Miyuki 11° SEED bead, second color,
    150 beads

B = 3 mm Fire-polished crystals,
    12 crystals

T = Tila Beads ,
    24 beads

Round 1 - V1 and V2

Pick up 12A, go with thread forward through the 1st A bead. Continue with thread around through all 12 A beads again coming out with thread at the 1st A bead.

Round 1

Round 2 - V1 and V2

a) Pick up 3A, go with thread right to left through 3 A beads in R1, as shown.

b) Repeat (a) around 5 more times.

c) Continue with working thread forward through the 1st A bead added at the first repeat of (a) in this Round.

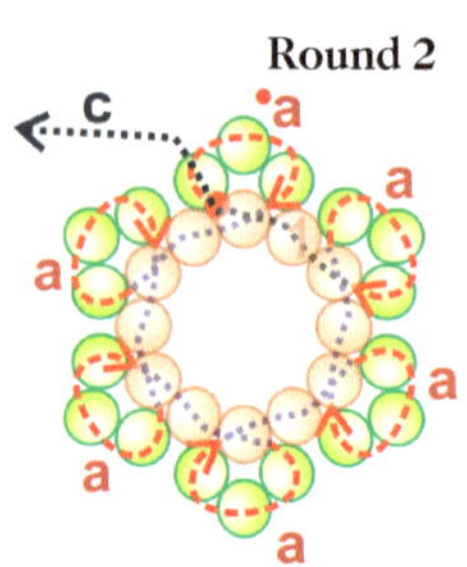

Round 3

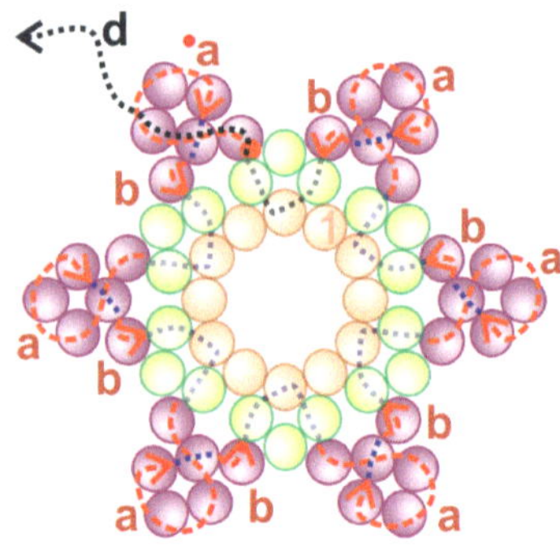

Round 3 - V1 and V2

a) Pick up 5A, go with thread forward through the 2nd A bead just added in this step.

b) Pick up 1A, go with thread down through the 3rd A bead, R2a, right to left through 1 A bead in R1, and up through the 1st A bead, R2a.

c) Repeat (a, b) around 5 more times.

d) Continue with working thread forward through the 1st, 2nd and 3rd A beads added at the first repeat of (a) in this Round.

Round 4 - V1 and V2
This Round is worked Clockwise

a) Pick up 4R, 1A, 2R, 1A, 2R, 1A, 2R, 1A, 2R, 1A, 2R, 1A, 4R, go with thread down through the 5th A bead, R3a.

I used 2 different colors of seed beads for this step (A and R) It is easier with the 2 colors to help not getting mixed up in the next step.

b) Pick up 2A, go with thread left to right through the 2nd A bead, R2a.

c) Pick up 2A, go with thread up through the 3rd A bead, R3a.

d) Repeat (a, b, c) around 5 more times.

e) Continue with thread up through the 4 R, 1 A and 2 R beads added in the first repeat of (a) in this round.

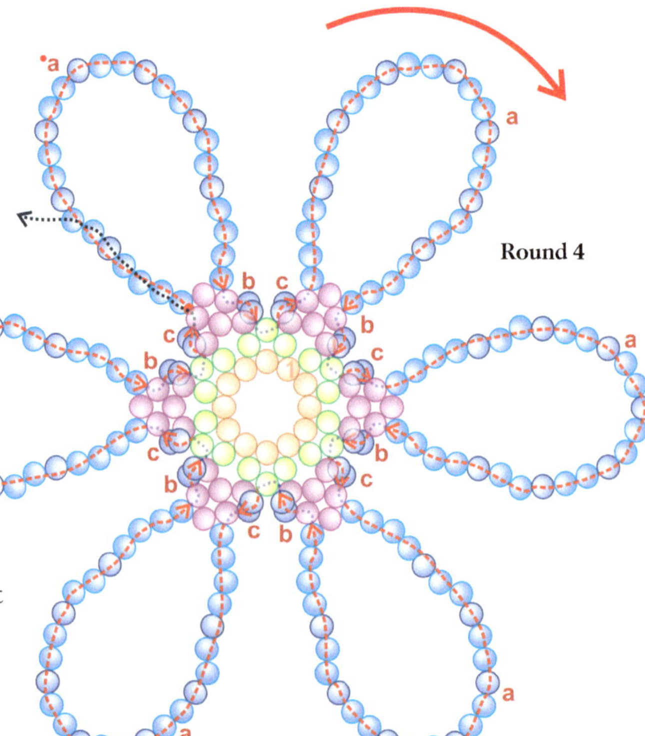

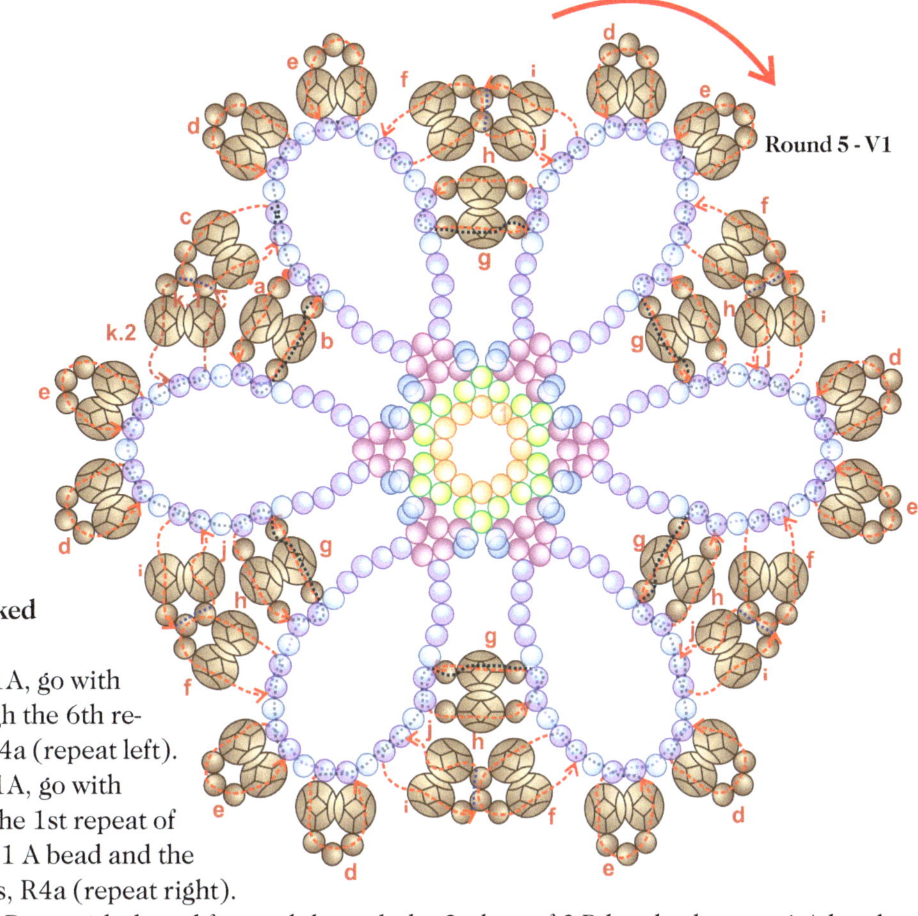

Round 5 - V1
This Round is worked Clockwise

a) Pick up 1A, 1B, 1A, go with thread down through the 6th repeat of 2R beads, R4a (repeat left).

b) Pick up 1A, 1B, 1A, go with thread up through the 1st repeat of 2 R beads, the next 1 A bead and the 2nd set of 2 R beads, R4a (repeat right).

c) Pick up 1B, 3A, 1B, go with thread forward through the 2nd set of 2 R beads, the next 1 A bead and the 3rd set of 2 R beads, R4a.

d) Pick up 1B, 3A, 1B, go with thread forward through the 3rd set of 2 R beads, the next 1 A bead and the 4th set of 2 R beads, R4a.

e) Pick up 1B, 3A, 1B, go with thread forward through the 4th set of 2 R beads, the next 1 A bead and the 5th set of 2 R beads, R4a.

f) Pick up 1B, 3A, 1B, go with thread forward through the 5th set of 2 R beads, the next 1 A bead and the 6th set of 2 R beads, R4a.

g) Pick up 1A, 1B, 1A, go with thread up through the 1st set of 2 R beads, R4a (repeat right).

h) Pick up 1A, 1B, 1A, go with thread down through the 6th repeat of 2 R beads, R4a (repeat left) left to right through the beads added in this Round at (g), up through 1st set of 2 R beads, the next 1 A bead and the 2nd set of 2 R beads, R4a.

i) Pick up 1B, 1A, go with thread down through the 2nd and 1st A beads added in this round at (f).

j) Pick up 1B, go with thread forward through the 2nd set of 2 R beads, the next 1 A bead and the 3rd set of 2 R beads, R4a.

k) Repeat (d, e, f, g, h, i, j) around 4 more times.
Repeat (d, e) 1 time.

k.1) Pick 1B, go with thread up through the 3rd and 2nd A beads added in this Round at (c).

k.2) Pick 1A, 1B, go with thread down through the 5th set of 2 R beads, up through the B bead added at (k.1), and left to right through the 3 A beads added in this Round at (c).

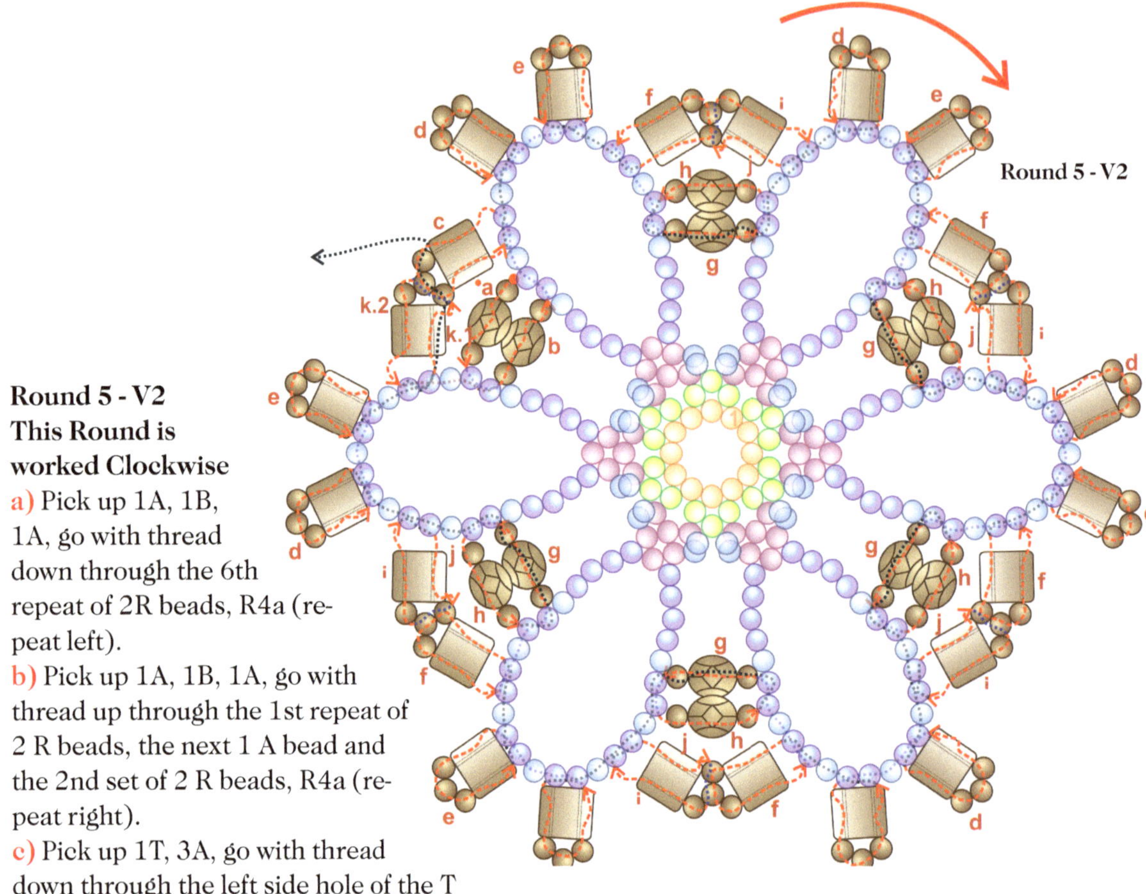

Round 5 - V2
This Round is worked Clockwise

a) Pick up 1A, 1B, 1A, go with thread down through the 6th repeat of 2R beads, R4a (repeat left).

b) Pick up 1A, 1B, 1A, go with thread up through the 1st repeat of 2 R beads, the next 1 A bead and the 2nd set of 2 R beads, R4a (repeat right).

c) Pick up 1T, 3A, go with thread down through the left side hole of the T bead, forward through the 2nd set of 2 R beads, the next 1 A bead and the 3rd set of 2 R beads, R4a.

d) Pick up 1T 3A, go with thread down through the left side hole of the T bead, forward through the 3rd set of 2 R beads, the next 1 A bead and the 4th set of 2 R beads, R4a.

e) Pick up 1T, 3A, go with thread down through the left side hole of the T bead, forward through the 4th set of 2 R beads, the next 1 A bead and the 5th set of 2 R beads, R4a.

f) Pick up 1T, 3A, go with thread down through the left side hole of the T bead, forward through the 5th set of 2 R beads, the next 1 A bead and the 6th set of 2 R beads, R4a.

g) Pick up 1A, 1B, 1A, go with thread up through the 1st set of 2 R beads, R4a (repeat right).

h) Pick up 1A, 1B, 1A, go with thread down through the 6th repeat of 2 R beads, R4a (repeat left) left to right through the beads added in this Round at (g), up through 1st set of 2 R beads, the next 1 A bead and the 2nd set of 2 R beads, R4a.

i) Pick up 1T, 1A, go with thread down through the 2nd and 1st A beads added in this round at (f).

j) Continue with working thread down through the left side hole of the T bead added in the last step, forward through the 2nd set of 2 R beads, the next 1 A bead and the 3rd set of 2 R beads, R4a.

k) Repeat (d, e, f, g, h, i, j) around 4 more times.

Repeat (d, e) 1 time.

k.1) Pick 1T, go with thread up through the 3rd and 2nd A beads added in this Round at (c).

k.2) Pick 1A,, go with thread down through the left side hole of the T bead added in the last step, forward through the 5th set of 2 R beads, up through the right side hole of the T bead added at (k.1), and left to right through the 3 A beads added in this Round at (c).

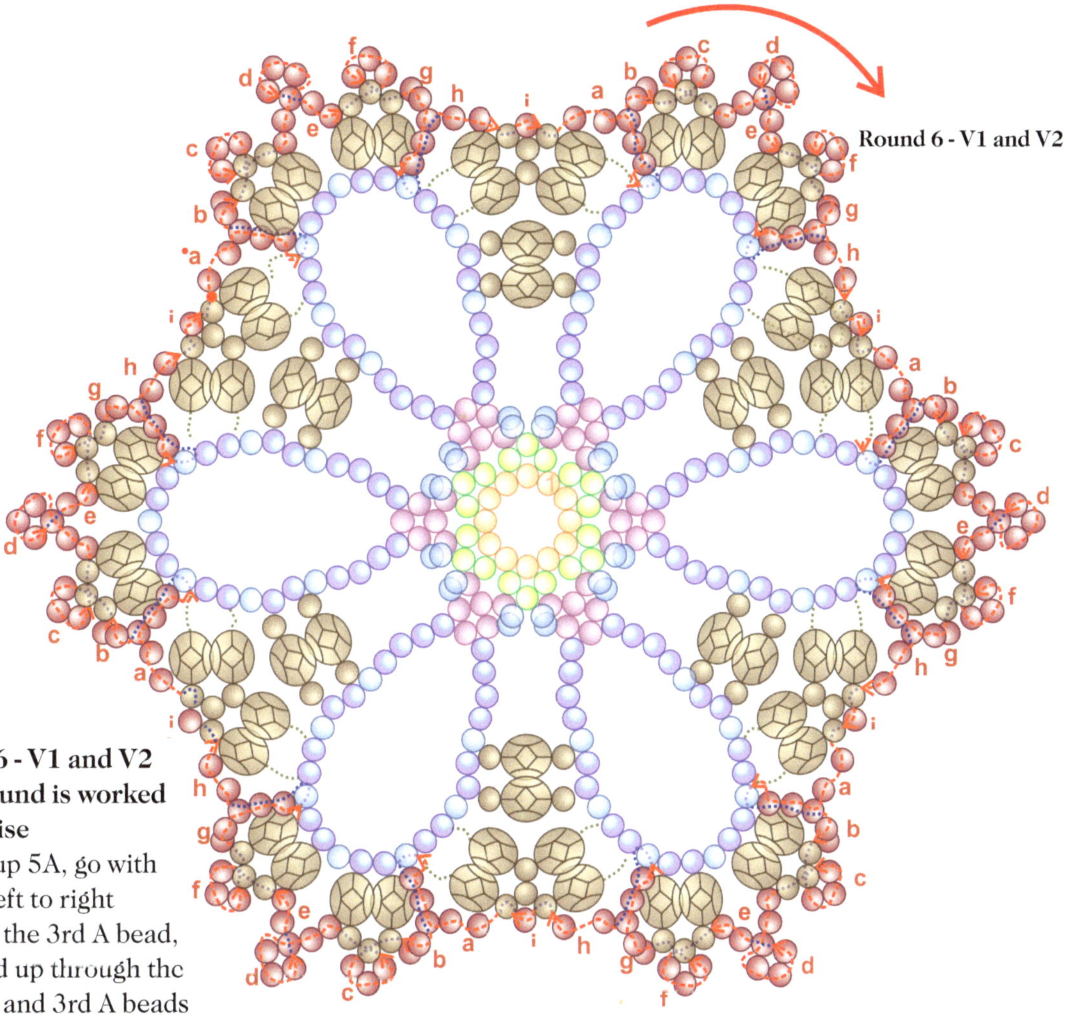

Round 6 - V1 and V2

Round 6 - V1 and V2
This Round is worked Clockwise

a) Pick up 5A, go with thread left to right through the 3rd A bead, R4a, and up through the 5th, 4th and 3rd A beads just added in this step.

b) Pick up 2A, go with thread left to right through the 3rd and 2nd A beads, R5d.

c) Pick up 3A, go with thread left to right through the 2nd and 1st A beads, R5d.

d) Pick up 6A, go with thread forward through the 3rd A bead just added.

e) Pick up 2A, go with thread left to right through the 3rd and 2nd A beads, R5e.

f) Pick up 3A, go with thread left to right through the 2nd and 1st A beads, R5e.

g) Pick up 5A, go with thread left to right through the 5th A bead, R4a, and up through the 5th, 4th and 3rd A beads just added.

h) Pick up 2A, go with thread left to right through the 3rd A bead, R5f.

i) Pick up 1A, go with thread left to right through the 1 A bead, R5i, or the 1st A bead, 5c.

j) Repeat (a, b, c, d, e, f, g, h, i) around 5 more times.

k) Weave the working thread into the snowflake and end.

When stiffening this snowflake, push these 2 Tila beads forward for dimension.

Lustrous Snowflake Ornament

Glow Snowflake Ornament

Shimmer Snowflake Ornament
4 Inches

1 Version
A = Miyuki 11° SEED bead,
      900 beads, I used a random combination of color beads
B = 3 mm Fire-polished crystals,
      6 crystals
E = Miyuki 8° SEED bead,
      18 beads

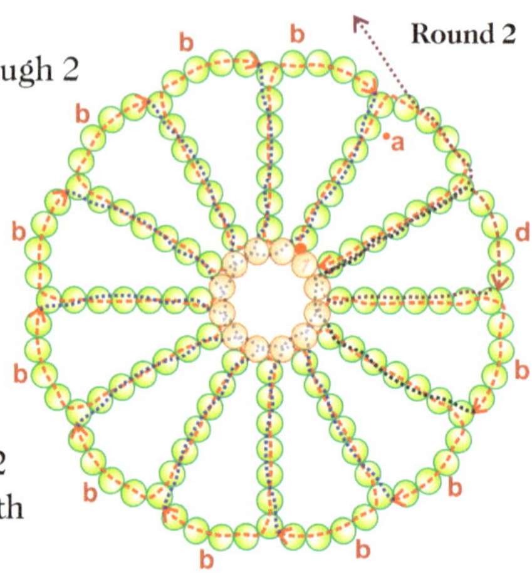

Round 1

Pick up 12A, go with thread forward through the 1st A bead. Continue with thread around through all 12 A beads again coming out with thread at the 1st A bead.

Round 2

a) Pick up 18A, go with thread right to left through 2 A beads in R1, as shown.

b) Pick up 11A, go with thread down through 7th though 1st A beads added in the last step and right to left through 2 A beads in R1, as shown.

c) Repeat (b) around 9 more times. After completing the last repeat of (b) continue with working thread up through the 18th through 12th A beads added at (a).

d) Pick up 4A, go with thread down through the 7th through 1st A beads added in the last repeat of (b), right to left through the 2 A beads in R1 as shown, up and then right to left through the 18th through 8th A beads added in (a) in this Round.

Round 3

a) Pick up 1E, go with thread right to left through the 11th, 10th, 9th and 8th A beads, R2a, R2b, or R2d.

b) Repeat (a) around 11 more times.

c) Continue with working thread forward through the 1 E bead added at the first repeat of (a) in this Round.

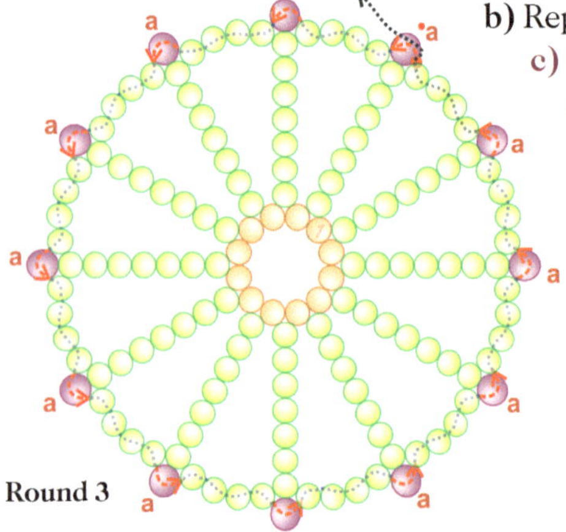

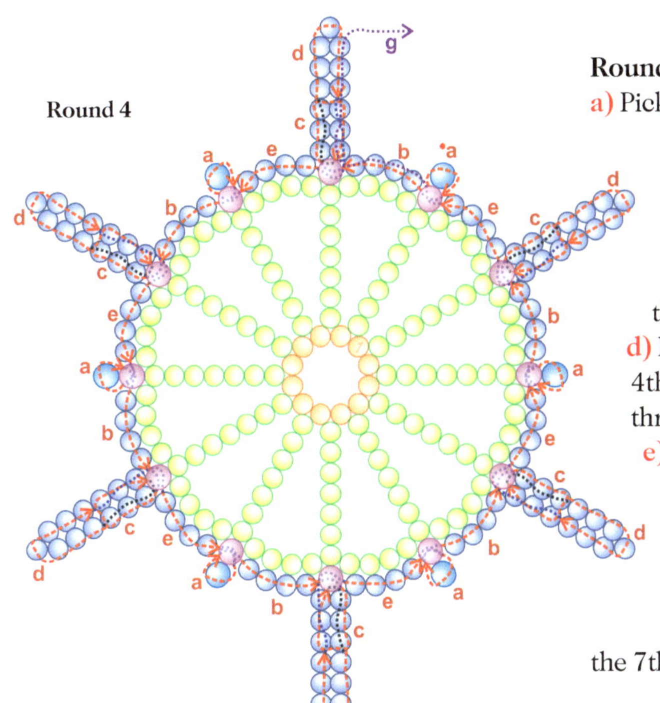

Round 4

a) Pick up 1E, go with thread right to left through the 1 E bead, R3a.

   b) Pick up 4A, go with thread right to left through the 1 E bead, R3a.

   c) Pick up 6A, go with thread right to left through the 1 E bead, R3a and up through the 1st, 2nd and 3rd A beads just added.

d) Pick up 7A, go with thread down through the 4th, 5th and 6th added at (c) and right to left through the 1 E bead, R3a.

   e) Pick up 4A, go with thread right to left through the 1 E bead, R3a.

   f) Repeat (a, b, c, d, e) around 5 more times.

   g) Continue with thread up through the 6th, 5th and 4th A beads added at (c) and the 7th, 6th and 5th A beads added at (d).

Round 5

a) Pick up 5A, go with thread right to left through the 5th and 4th A beads, R4d.

b) Pick up 7A, go with thread right to left through the 4th and 3rd A beads, R4d.

c) Pick up 5A, go with thread down through the 3rd, 2nd and 1st A beads, R4d and the 3rd, 2nd and 1st A beads, R4c and right to left through the 1st, 2nd and 3rd A beads, R4e.

d) Pick up 3A, go with thread right to left through the 1 E bead, R4a.

e) Pick up 4A, go with thread right to left through the 3rd A bead added at (d), the 1 E bead, R4a and the 1st A bead just added in this step.

f) Pick up 2A, go with thread right to left through the 2nd, 3rd and 4th A beads, R4b, up through 6th, 5th and 4th A beads added at R4c and the 7th, 6th and 5th A beads added at R4d.

g) Repeat (a, b, c, d, e, f) around 5 more times.

h) Continue with working thread forward through the 1st, 2nd and 3rd A beads added in the first repeat of (a) in this Round.

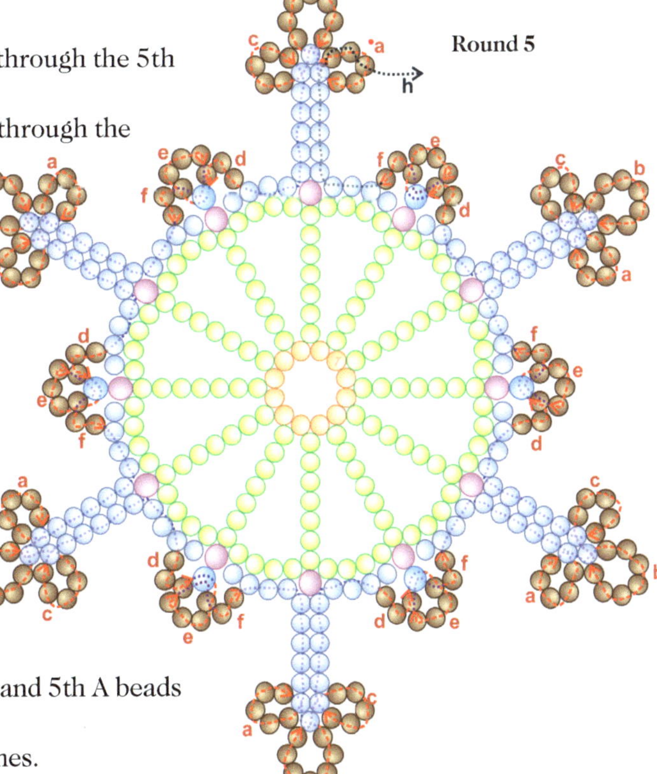

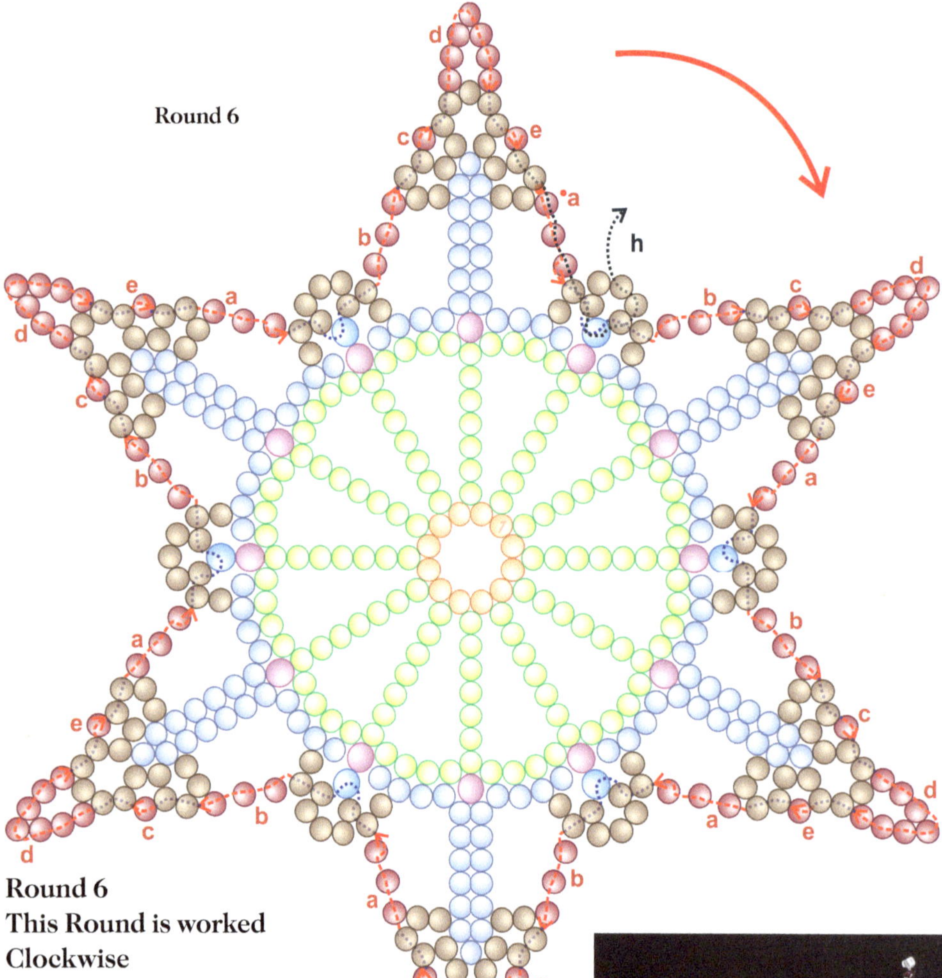

Round 6
This Round is worked Clockwise

a) Pick up 3A, go with thread left to right through the 1st A bead, R5f, the 1st A bead, R5e, the 1 E bead, R4a and the 3rd and 2nd A beads, R5d.

b) Pick up 3A, go with thread up through the 3rd and 4th A beads, R5c.

c) Pick up 1A, go with thread up through the 2nd and 3rd A beads, R5b.

d) Pick up 7A, go with thread down through the 5th and 6th A beads, R5b.

e) Pick up 1A, go with thread down through the 2nd and 3rd A beads, R5a.

f) Repeat (a, b, c, d, e around 5 more times.

g) After repeating the last repeat of (e), continue with working thread right to left through the 4th and 3rd A beads in Round 5 at (e). Follow thread path in illustration.

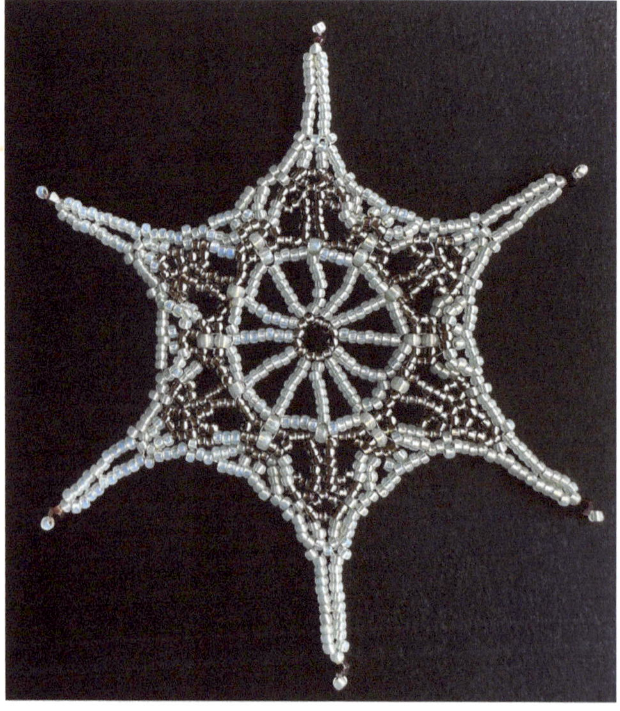

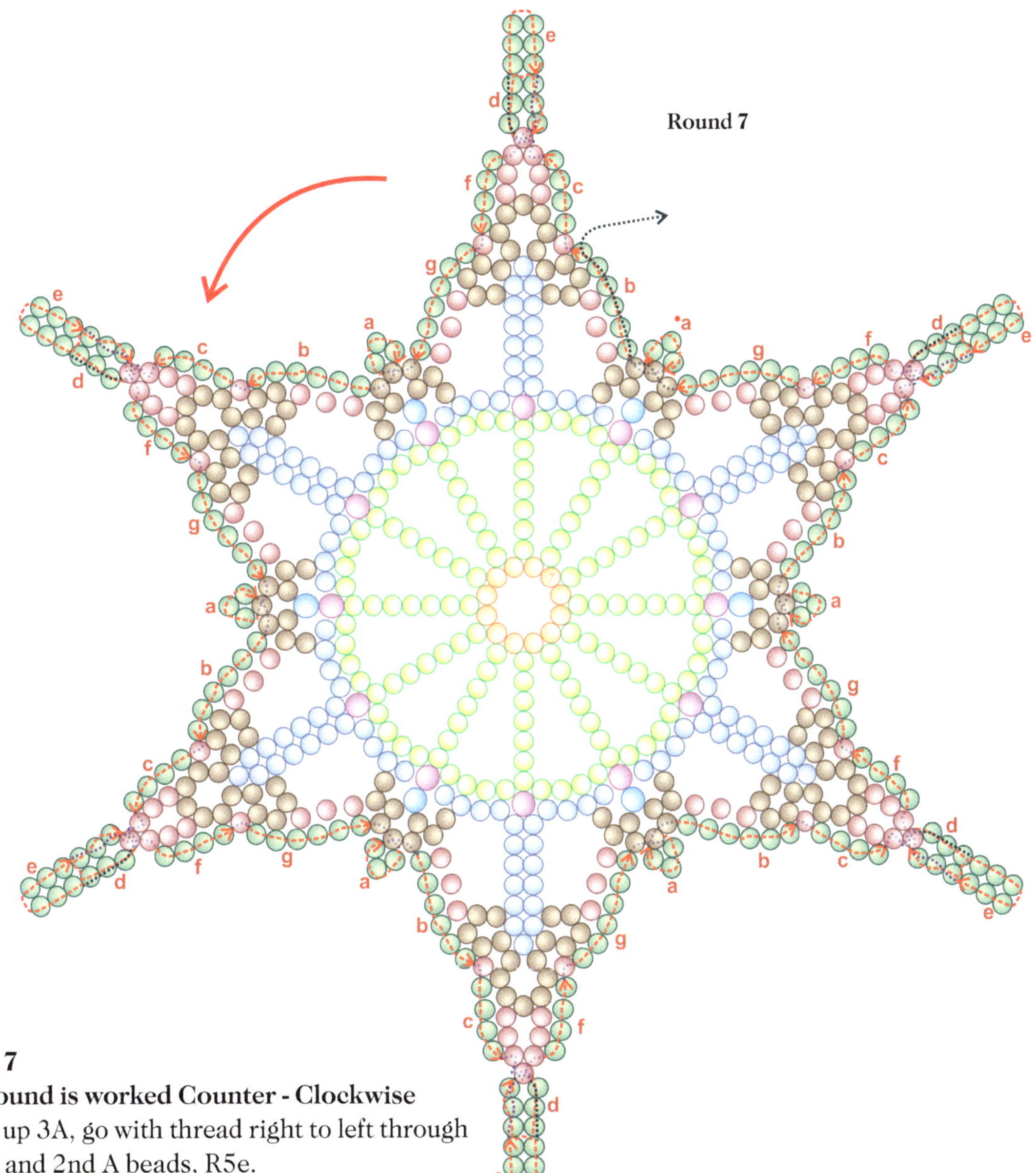

Round 7

This Round is worked Counter - Clockwise

a) Pick up 3A, go with thread right to left through the 3rd and 2nd A beads, R5e.

b) Pick up 6A, go with thread up through the 1 A bead, R6e.

c) Pick up 4A, go with thread up through the 5th and 4th A beads, R6d.

d) Pick up 6A, go with thread right to left through the 4th A bead, R6d and up through the 1st, 2nd and 3rd A beads just added in this step.

e) Pick up 6A, go with thread down through the 4th, 5th and 6th A beads added at (d), right to left through the 4th and 3rd A beads, R6d.

f) Pick up 4A, go with thread down through the 1 A bead, R6c.

g) Pick up 6A, go with thread right to left through the 4th and 3rd A beads, R5e.

h) Repeat (a, b, c, d, e, f, g) around 5 more times.

i) Continue with working thread forward through the 6 A beads added in the first repeat of (b) in this Round.

Round 8

a) Pick up 1A, go with thread up through the 4 A beads, R7c.

b) Pick up 1A, go with thread up through the 6th, 5th and 4th A beads, R7d and the 6th, 5th, 4th A beads, R7e.

c) Pick up 5A, 1B, 1A, go with thread down through the B bead and the 5th A bead just added.

d) Pick up 4A, go with thread down through the 3rd, 2nd and 1st A bead, R7e and the 3rd, 2nd and 1st A beads, R7d.

e) Pick up 1A, go with thread down through the 4 A beads, R7f.

f) Pick up 1A, go with thread down through the 1st and 2nd A beads, R7g..

g) Pick up 3A, go with thread right to left through the 2nd A bead, R7a.

h) Pick up 3A, go with thread up through the 5th and 6th A beads, R7b.

i) Repeat (a, b, c, d, e, f, g, h) around 5 more times.

j) Weave the working thread into the snow-flake and end.

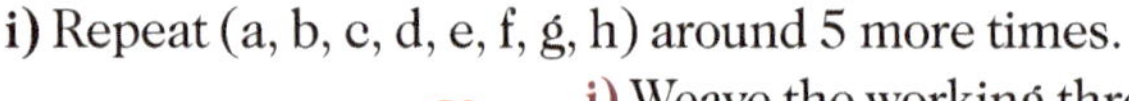

Stopping after Round 6

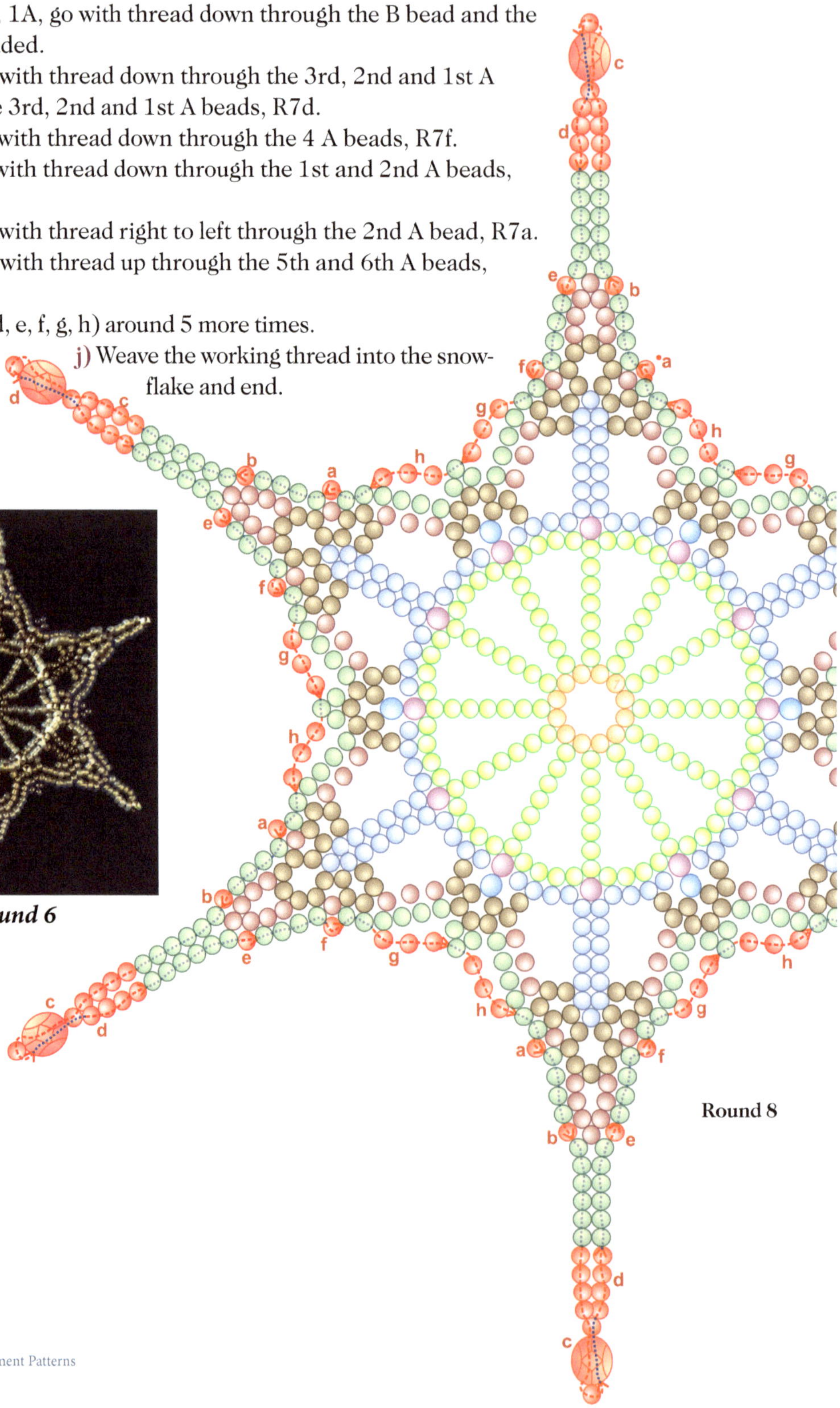

Round 8

Sparkling Snowflake Ornament
2-1/2 Inches

Version 1

A = Miyuki 11° SEED bead,
570 beads
B = 3 mm Fire-polished crystals,
30 crystals
C = 4 mm Fire-polished crystals,
12 crystals

Version 2

A = Miyuki 11° SEED bead,
570 beads
C = 4 mm Fire-polished crystals,
12 crystals
D = DiamonDuo beads,
12 beads

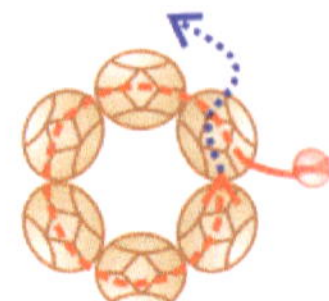

Round 1 - V1 and V2

Pick up 6B, go with thread forward through the 1st B bead. Continue with thread around through all 6 B beads again coming out with thread at the 1st B bead.

Round 2 - V1

a) Pick up 6A, 1B, 2A, 1B, 2A, go with thread forward through the 1st B bead just added in this step.
b) Pick up 6A, go with thread right to left through the 2 B beads in R1 as shown.
c) Repeat (a, b) around 5 more times.
d) Continue with working thread up through the 1st and 2nd A beads added in the first repeat of (a) this Round.

Round 2 - V2

a) Pick up 6A, 1D, 6A, go with thread right to left through the 2 B beads in R1 as shown.
b) Repeat (a) around 5 more times.
c) Continue with working thread up through the 1st and 2nd A beads added in the first repeat of (a) this Round.

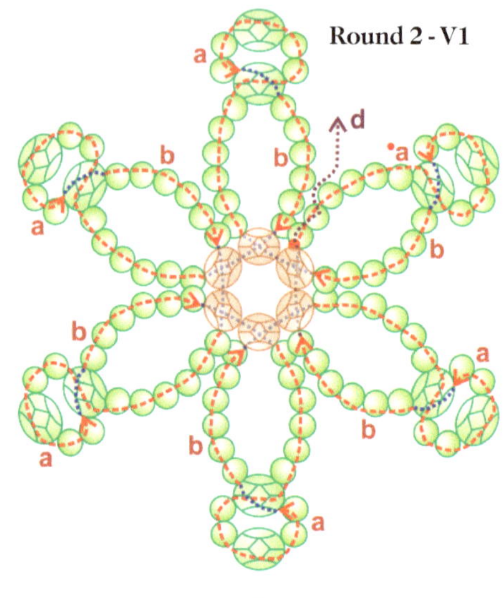

Round 2 - V1

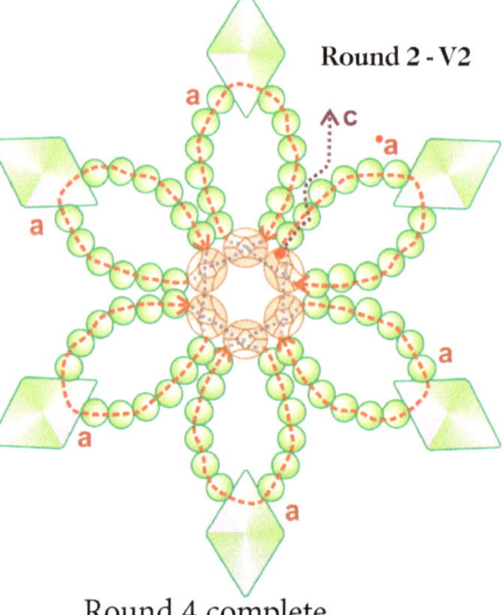

Round 2 - V2

Round 4 complete

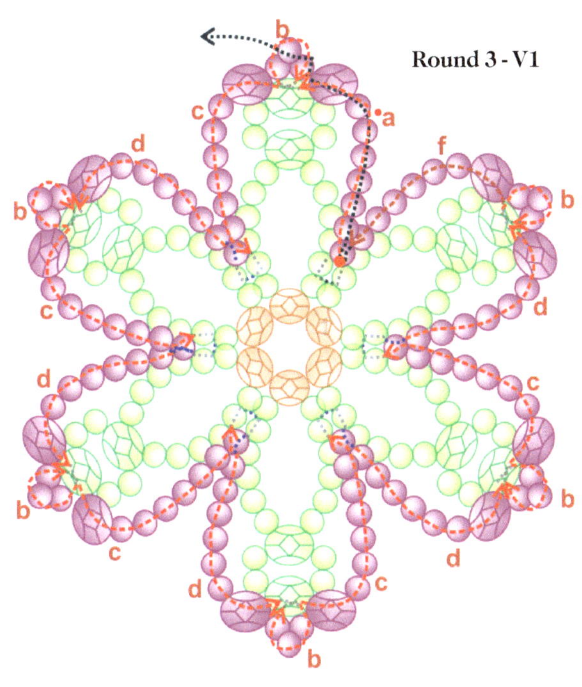

Round 3 - V1 and V2

a) Pick up 7A, 1B, go with thread right to left through the 2nd B bead or the top hole of the D bead, R2a.

b) Pick up 3A, go with thread right to left through the 2nd B bead or the top hole of the D bead, R2a.

c) Pick up 1B, 7A, go with thread down through the 2nd A bead, R2a, up through the 5th A bead, R2b, or the 2nd set of A beads, R2a-v2, and the 7th A bead just added in this step.

d) Pick up 6A, 1B, go with thread right to left through the 2nd B bead, R2a, or the top hole of the D bead, R2a-v2.

e) Repeat (b, c, d) around 4 more times.

Repeat (b) 1 time.

f) Pick up 1B, 6A, go with thread down through the 1st A bead added at (a), down through the 2nd A bead, R2a, up through the 5th A bead, R2b, or the 2nd set of A beads, R2a-v2, and the 1st through 7th A beads and the B bead added at (a) and right to left through the 3rd and 2nd A beads added in this step at the first repeat of (b).

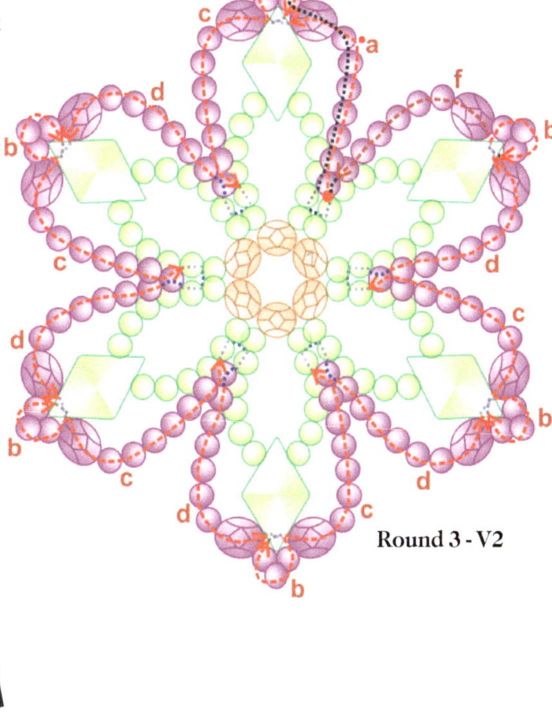

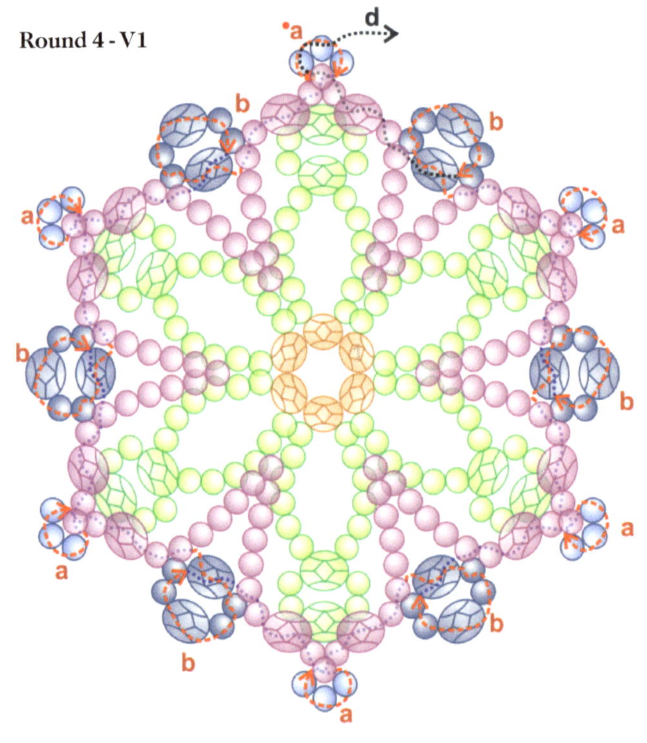

Round 4 - V1

Round 4 - V1

a) Pick up 3A, go with thread right to left through the 2nd and 1st A beads, R3b, the B bead and 1st and 2nd A beads, R3c.

b-V1) Pick up 1B, 2A, 1B, 2A, go with thread right to left through the 1st B bead just added in this step, the 6th and 7th A beads, R3a or the 5th and 6th A beads, R3d, the B bead, R3a or R3d, and the 3rd and 2nd A beads, R3b.

b-V2) Pick up 1D, go with thread right to left through the 6th and 7th A beads, R3a or the 5th and 6th A beads, R3d, the B bead, R3a or R3d, and the 3rd and 2nd A beads, R3b.

c) Repeat (a, b) around 5 more times.

d) Continue with working thread through the 1st and 2nd A beads added in this step at the first repeat of (a).

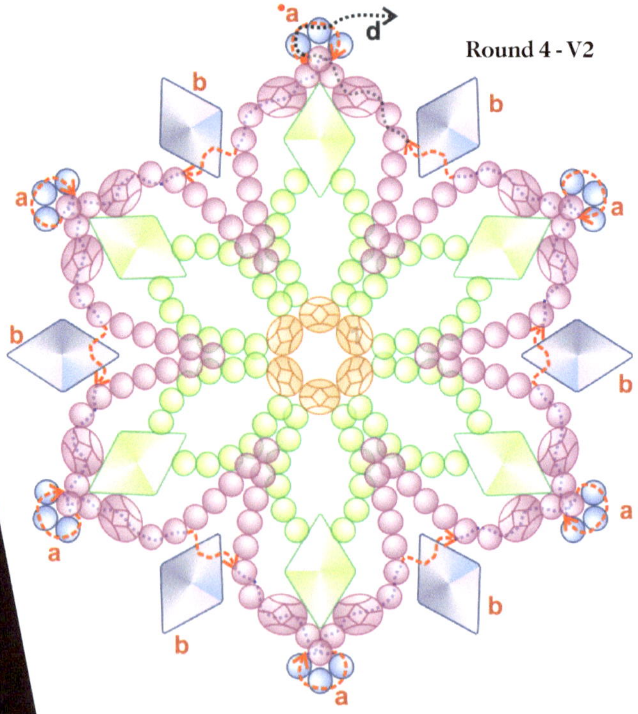

Round 4 - V2

Round 5 - V1 and V2
This Round is worked Clockwise

a) Pick up 3A, go with thread left to right through the 2nd A bead, R4a.

b) Pick up 6A, go with thread left to right through the 2nd B bead or the top hole of the D bead, R4b.

c) Pick up 6A, go with thread left to right through the 2nd A bead, R4a.

d) Repeat (a, b, c) around 5 more times.

e) Continue with working thread forward through the 1st and 2nd A beads added in the first repeat of (a) in this Round.

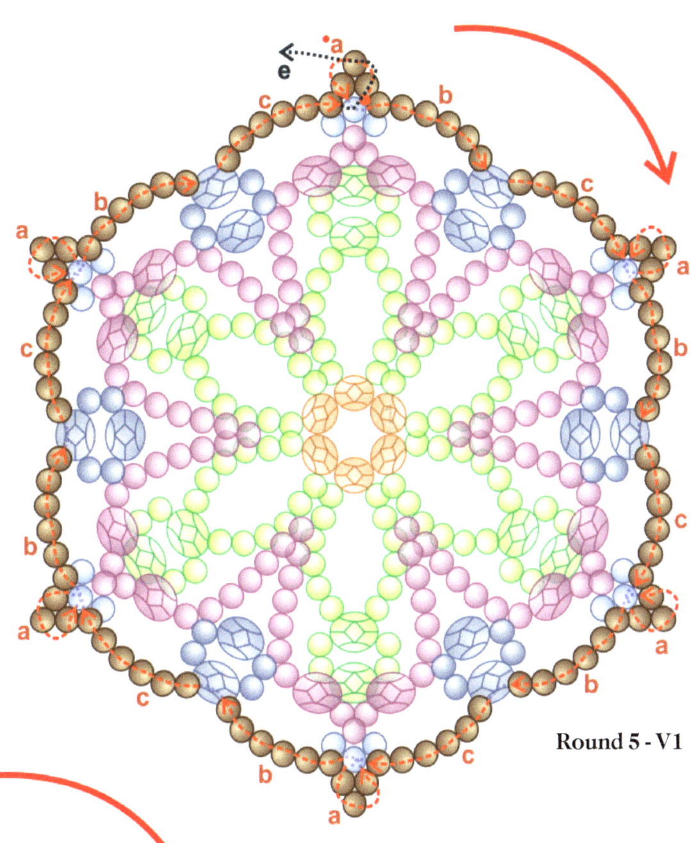

Round 5 - V1

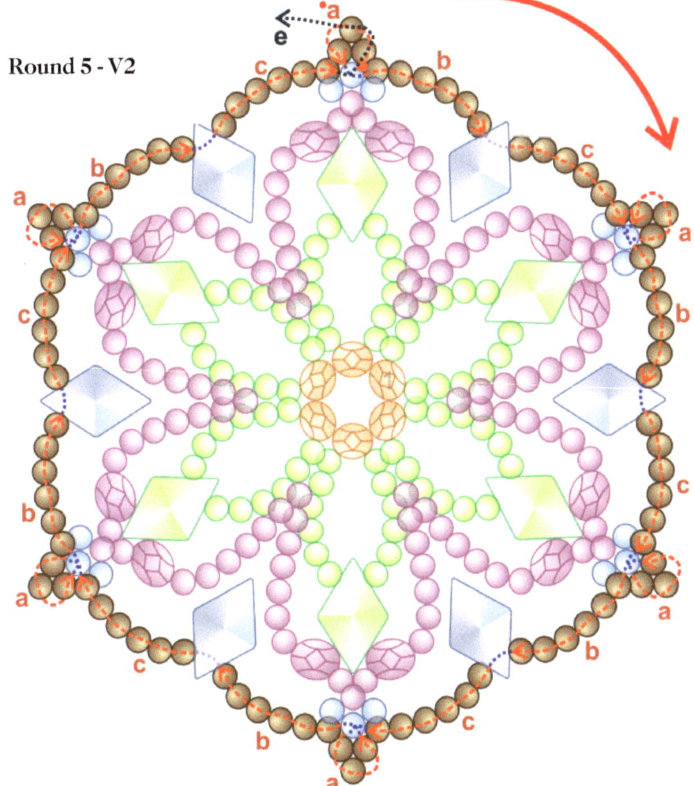

Round 5 - V2

Round 6 - V1 and V2
This Round is worked Counter - Clockwise

a) Pick up 3A, go with thread right to left through the 2nd A bead, R5a.

b) Pick up 3A, go with thread right to left through the 5th A bead, R5c.

c) Pick up 1C, 7A, go with thread left to right through the 6th A bead, R5b, the 2nd B bead or the top hole of the D bead, R4b, and through the 1st A bead, R5c.

d) Pick up 2A, go with thread right to left through the 5th A bead added in this Round at (c).

e) Pick up 4A, 1C, go with thread right to left through the 2nd A bead, R5b.

f) Pick up 3A, go with thread right to left through the 2nd A bead, R5a.

g) Repeat (a, b, c, d, e, f) around 5 more times.

h) Continue with working thread forward through the 1st and 2nd A beads added in the first repeat of (a) in this Round.

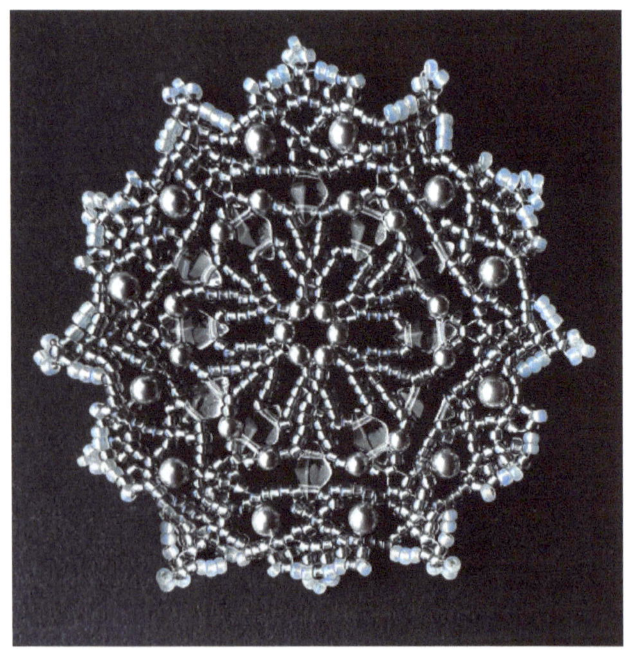

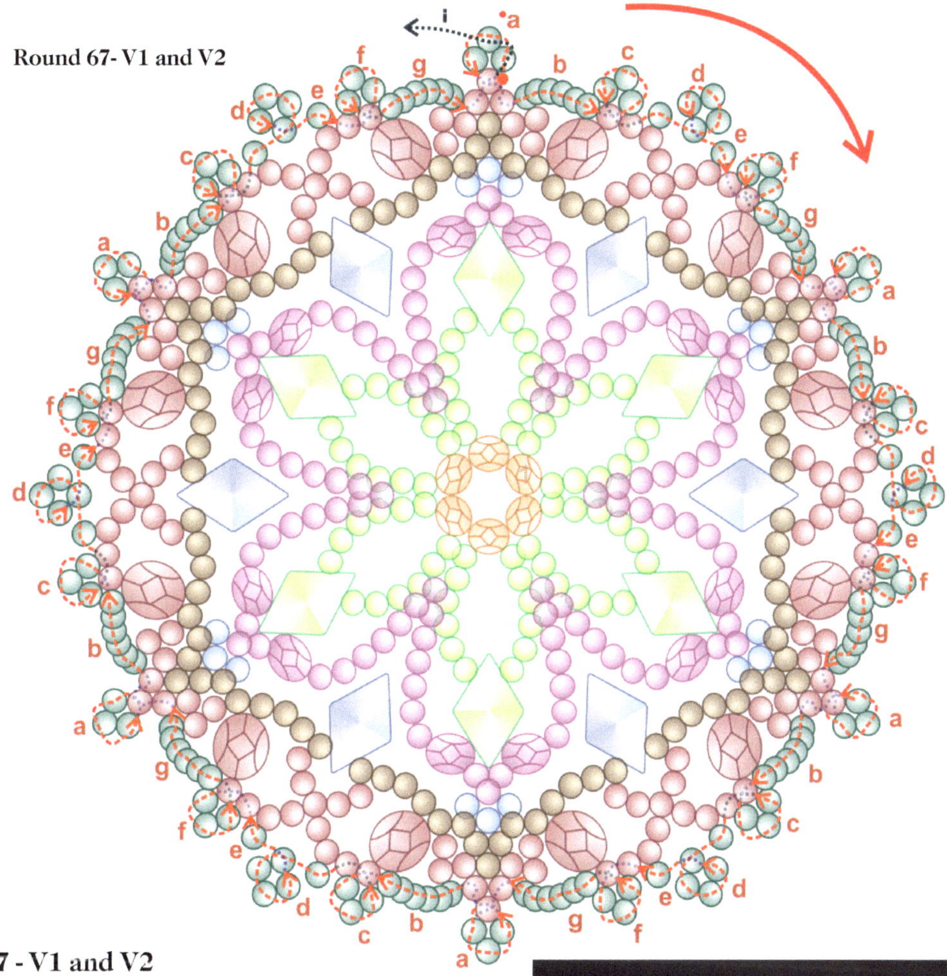

Round 7 - V1 and V2
This Round is worked Clockwise

a) Pick up 3A, go with thread left to right through the 2nd and 3rd A beads, R6a.

b) Pick up 6A, go with thread left to right through the 4th A bead, R6e.

c) Pick up 3A, go with thread left to right through the 4th and 3rd A beads, R6e.

d) Pick up 5A, go with thread forward through the 2nd A bead just added in this step.

e) Pick up 1A, go with thread left to right through the 2nd and 1st A beads, R6c.

f) Pick up 3A, go with thread left to right through the 1st A bead, R6c.

g) Pick up 6A, go with thread left to right through the 1st and 2nd A beads, R6a.

h) Repeat (a, b, c, d, e, f, g) around 5 more times.

i) Continue with working thread forward through the 1st and 2nd A beads added in the first repeat of (a) in this Round.

Round 8 - V1 and V2
This Round is worked Counter - Clockwise
a) Pick up 3A, go with right to left through the 2nd and 3rd A beads, R7a.

b) Pick up 3A, go with thread right to left through the 3rd, 2nd and 1st A beads, R7g, and the 1st A bead, R7f.

c) Pick up 1A, go with thread right to left through the 2nd A bead, R7f.

d) Pick up 2A, go with thread right to left through the 4th A bead, R7d.

e) Pick up 3A, go with thread right to left through the 4th A bead, R7d.

f) Pick up 2A, go with thread right to left through the 2nd A bead, R7c.

g) Pick up 1A, go with thread right to left through the 3rd A bead, R7c, and the 6th, 5th and 4th A beads, R7b.

h) Pick up 3A, go with thread up through the 1st and 2nd A beads, R7a.

i) Repeat (a, b, c, d, e, f, g, h) around 5 more times.

j) Weave the working thread into the snowflake and end.

Dazzling Snowflake Ornament
2-1/2 Inches

Version 1

A = Miyuki 11° SEED bead,
  800 beads

B = 3 mm Fire-polished crystals,
  24 beads

E = Miyuki 8° SEED bead,
  36 beads

F = Miyuki 15° SEED bead,
  90 beads

Version 2

A = Miyuki 11° SEED bead,
  800 beads

B = 3 mm Fire-polished crystals,
  6 beads

D = DiamonDuo beads,
  18 beads

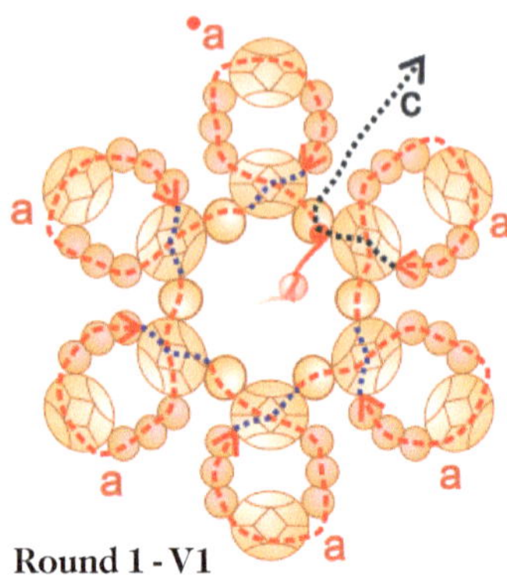

Round 1 - V1

Round 1 - V1

Round 1 - V1

a) Pick up 1A, 1B, 3F 1B, 3F, go with thread forward through the 1st B bead.
b) Repeat (a) around 5 more times.
c) Continue with thread around through all center beads again coming out with thread at the 1st A bead.

Round 1 - V2

a) Pick up 1A, 1D.
b) Repeat (a) around 5 more times.
c) Continue with thread around through all center beads again coming out with thread at the 1st A bead.

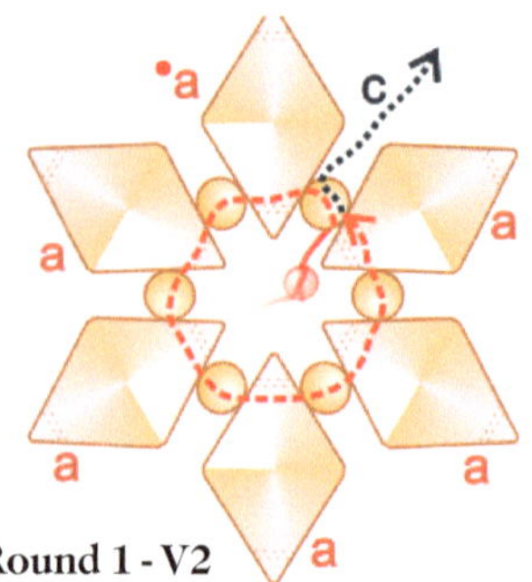

Round 1 - V2

Round 2 -V1 and V2

a) Pick up 8A, go with thread down through the 7th through 1st A beads just added and right to left through the 1 A, 1 B (or 1 D, bottom hole) and 1 A in R1 as shown.
b) Repeat (a) around 5 more times.
c) Continue with working thread up through the 8 A beads added at the first repeat of (a) in this Round.

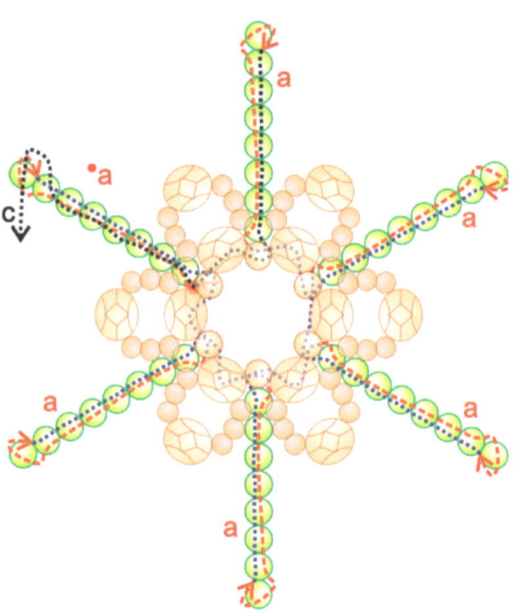

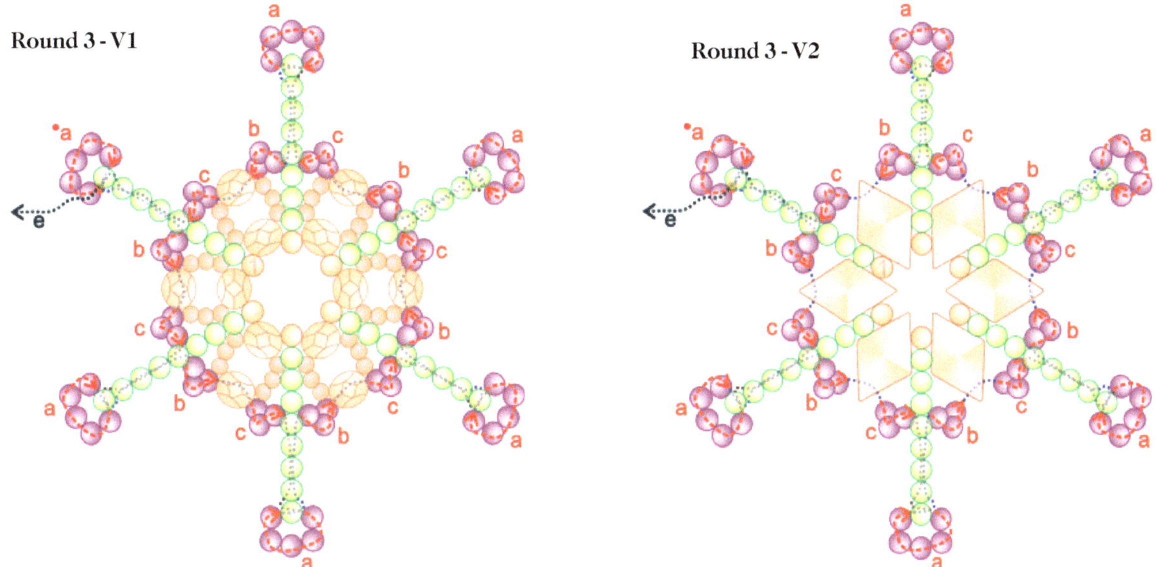

Round 3 - V1 and V2

a) Pick up 5A, go with thread right to left through the 8th A bead and down through the 7th, 6th, 5th and 4th A beads, R2a.

b) Pick up 3A, go with thread right to left through the 2nd B bead (V1) or the top hole of the D bead (V2), R1a.

c) Pick up 3A, go with thread up through the 4th, 5th, 6th and 7th A beads, R2a and right to left through the 8th A bead, R2a.

d) Repeat (a, b, c) around 5 more times.

e) Continue with working thread forward though the 1st A bead added at the first repeat of (a) in this Round.

Round 4 - V1 and V2

This Round is worked Clockwise

a) Pick up 3A, go with thread left to right through the 3rd A bead, R3a.

b) Pick up 3A, go with thread down through the 5th A bead, R3a.

c) Pick up 4A, go with thread left to right through the 2nd A bead, R3c.

d) Pick up 3A, go with thread left to right through the 2nd A bead, R3b.

e) Pick up 4A, go with thread up through the 1st A bead, R3a.

f) Repeat (a, b, c, d, e) around 5 more times. .

g) Continue with thread up through the 1st and 2nd A beads added in this Round at the first repeat of (a), as shown.

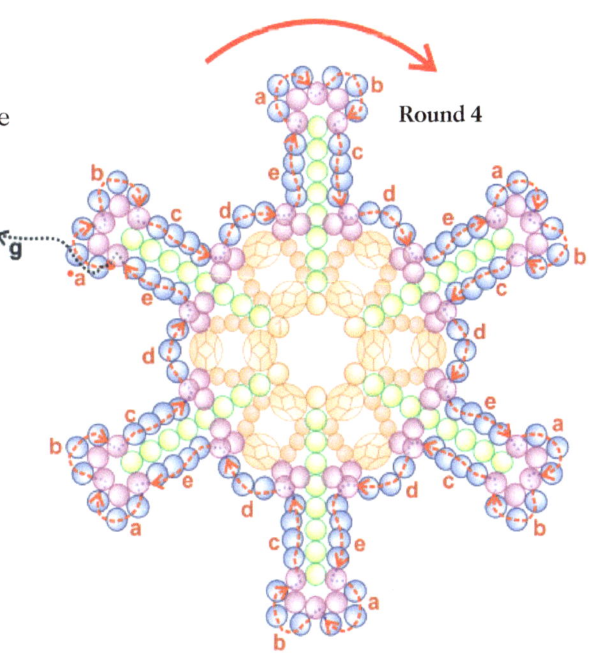

Round 5 - V1

This Round is worked Clockwise

a) Pick up 7A, 1E, 7A, go with thread left to right through the 3rd A bead, R4a.

b) Pick up 1A, go with thread left to right through the 1st A bead, R4b.

c) Pick up 7A, 1E, 7A, go with thread down through the 2nd and 3rd A beads, R4b.

d.1) Pick up 1B, 3F, 1B, 3F, go with thread left to right through the 1 B bead just added in this step.

d.2) Pick up 4A, go with thread left to right through the 2nd A bead, R4d.

e) Pick up 4A, 1B, 3F, 1B, 3F, go with thread left to right (forward) through the 1st B bead just added and up through the 1st and 2nd A beads, R4a.

f) Repeat (a, b, c, d, e) around 5 more times.

g) Continue with working thread up through the 1st through 5th A beads added in the first repeat of (a) in this Round.

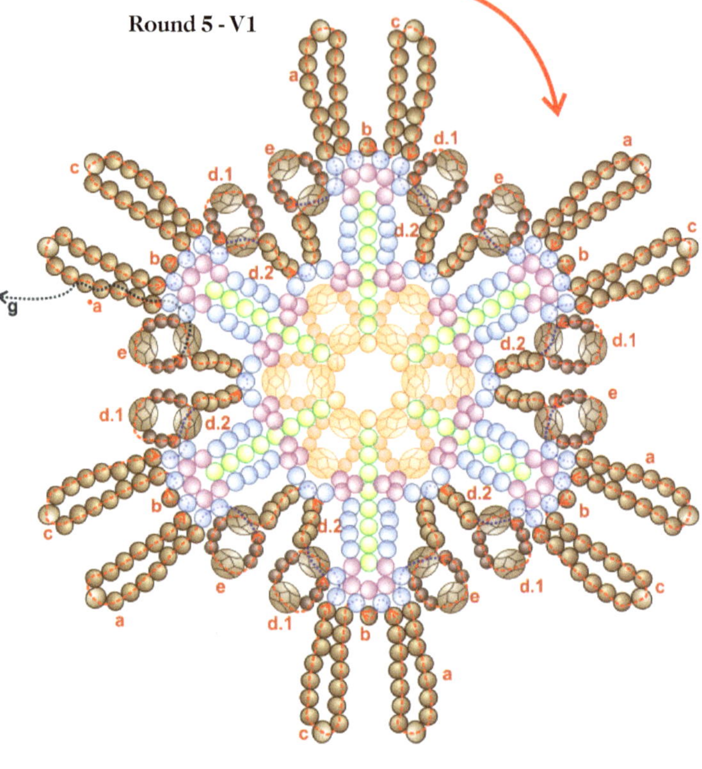

Round 5 - V2

This Round is worked Clockwise

a) Pick up 7A, 1E, 7A, go with thread left to right through the 3rd A bead, R4a.

b) Pick up 1A, go with thread left to right through the 1st A bead, R4b.

c) Pick up 7A, 1E, 7A, go with thread down through the 2nd and 3rd A beads, R4b.

d) Pick up 1D, 4A, go with thread left to right through the 2nd A bead, R4d.

e) Pick up 4A, 1D, go with thread up through the 1st and 2nd A beads, R4a.

f) Repeat (a, b, c, d, e) around 5 more times.

g) Continue with working thread up through the 1st through 5th A beads added in the first repeat of (a) in this Round.

Round 6 - V1 and V2
This Round is worked Clockwise

a) Pick up 3A, go with thread left to right through the 7th A bead, the E bead and the next A bead, R5a.

b) Pick up 1B, go with thread left to right through the 7th A bead and the E bead, R5c.

c) Pick up 9A, go with thread forward through the 6th A bead just added in this step.

d) Pick up 5A, go with thread left to right through the E bead and the next A bead, R5a, the B bead added in this Round at (b), the 7th A bead, the E bead and the next A bead, R5c.

e) Pick up 3A, go with thread down through the 3rd and 4th A beads (of the second set of 7A, R5c.

f) Pick up 3A, go with thread left to right through the 2nd B bead (V1) or the top hole of the D bead, R5d.

g) Pick up 4A, go with thread down through the 3rd A bead, R5d or R5d.2.

h) Pick up 1A, go with thread up through the 2nd A bead, R5e.

i) Pick up 1A, go with thread up through the 3rd A bead added in this Round at (g).

j) Pick up 2A, go with thread left to right through the 2nd B bead (V1) or the top hole of the D bead, R5e.

k) Pick up 3A, go with thread up through the 4th and 5th A beads, R5a.

l) Repeat (a, b, c, d, e, f, g, h, i, j, k) around 5 more times.

m) Weave the working thread into the snowflake and end.

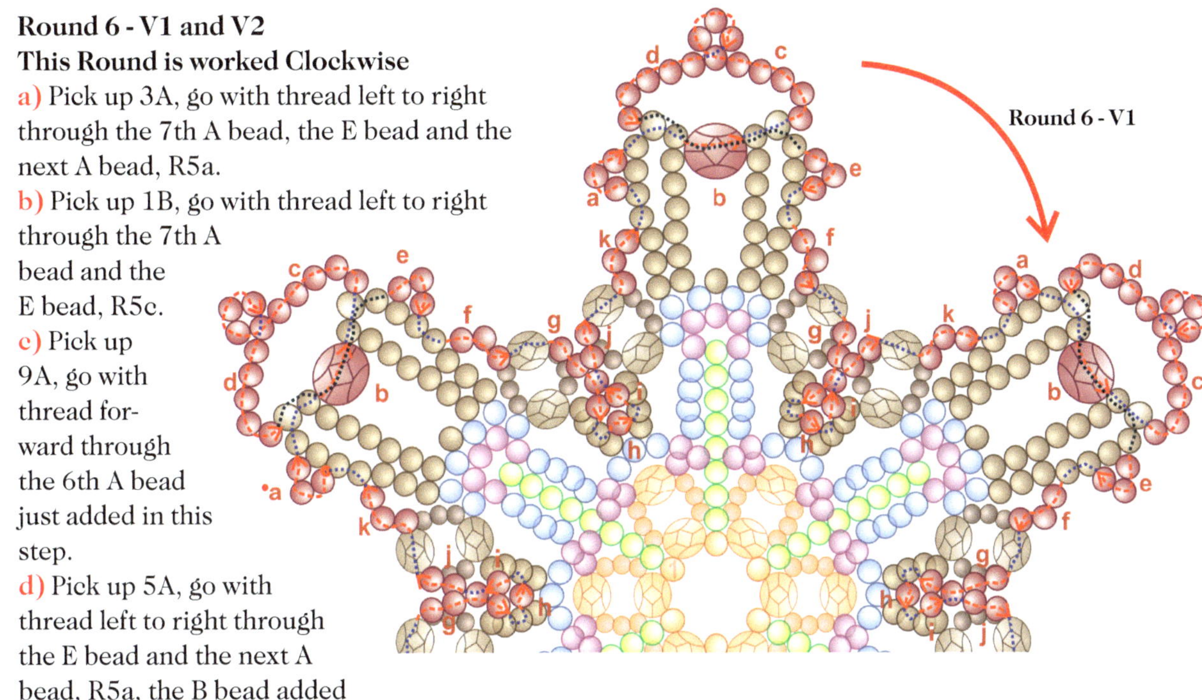

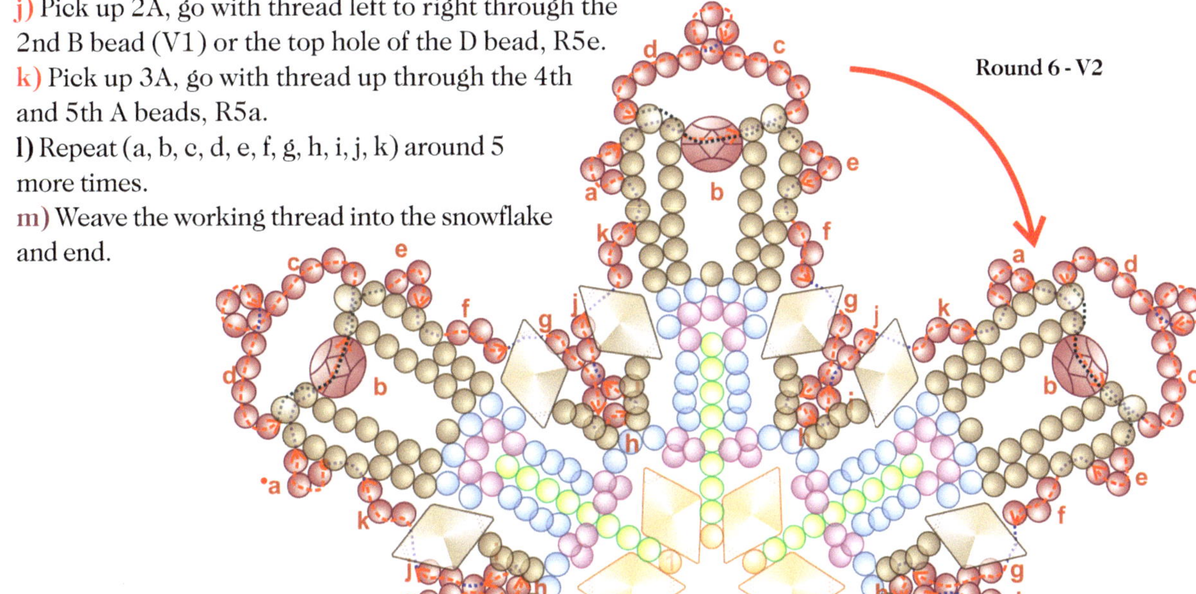

Dazzling Snowflake Pattern

Dazzling Snowflake Pattern

Joyful Snowflake Ornament

2 ¾ Inches

Version 1
A = Miyuki 11° SEED bead,
  580 beads
B = 3 mm Fire-polished crystals,
  36 crystals
C = 4 mm Fire-polished crystals,
  6 crystals
E = Miyuki 8° SEED bead,
  18 beads
F = Miyuki 15° SEED bead,
  108 beads

Version 2
A = Miyuki 11° SEED bead,
  580 beads
D = DiamondDuo Beads,
  30 beads

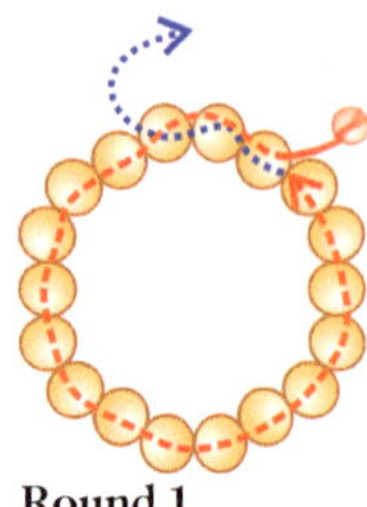

Round 1

Round 1 - V1 and V2

Pick up 18A, go with thread forward through the 1st A bead. Continue with thread around through all 18 A beads again coming out with thread at the 1st A bead.

Round 2 - V1

a.1) Pick up 8A, 1E, 3F, 1E, 1F, go with thread down through the 2nd F bead just added in this step.

a.2) Pick up 1F, go with thread left to right through 1st E bead added at (a.1).

a.3) Pick up 8A, go with thread right to left through 5 A beads in R1, as shown.

b) Repeat (a.1, a.2, a.3) around 5 more times.

c) Continue with working thread forward through the 1st, 2nd, 3rd and 4th A beads added at the first repeat of (a) in this Round.

Round 2 - V2

a) Pick up 8A, 1D, 8A, go with thread right to left through 5 A beads in R1, as shown.

b) Repeat (a) around 5 more times.

c) Continue with working thread forward through the 1st, 2nd, 3rd and 4th A beads added at the first repeat of (a) in this Round.

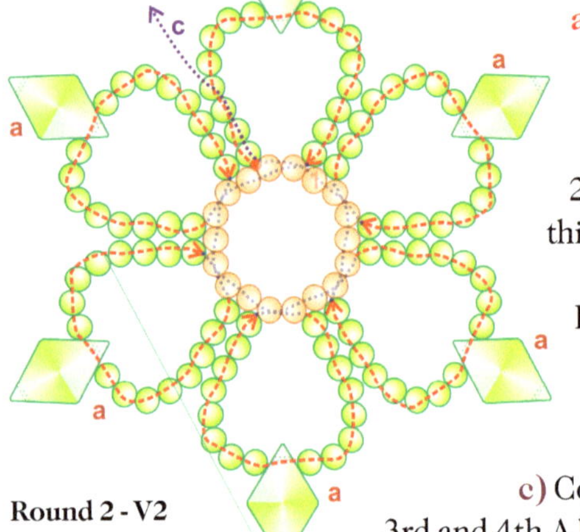

Round 2 - V2

Round 2 - V1

Round 3 - V1 and V2

a) Pick up 1A, go with thread down through 5th, 6th and 7th A beads (of the second set of 8A), R2a or the 8 A beads, R2a.3.

b) Pick up 2A, go with thread up through 2nd, 3rd and 4th A beads (of the first set of 8A), R2a or the 8 A beads, R2a.1.

c) Repeat (a, b) around 5 more times.

d) Continue with working thread forward through the 1 A bead added at the first repeat of (a) in this Round.

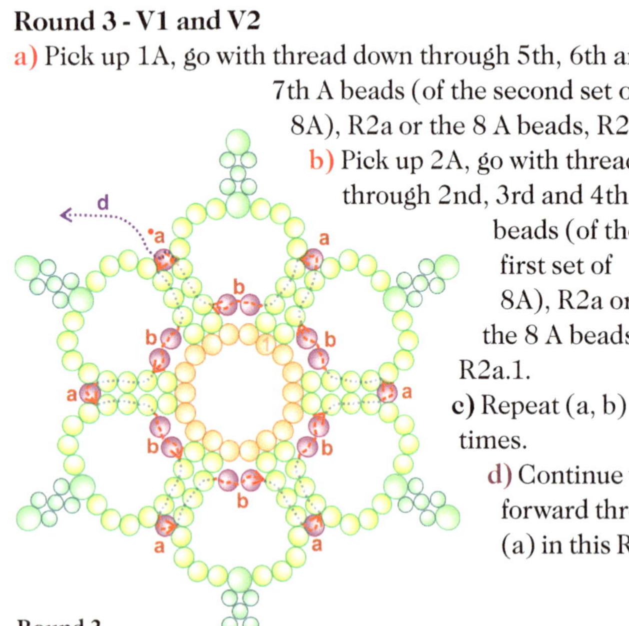

Round 3

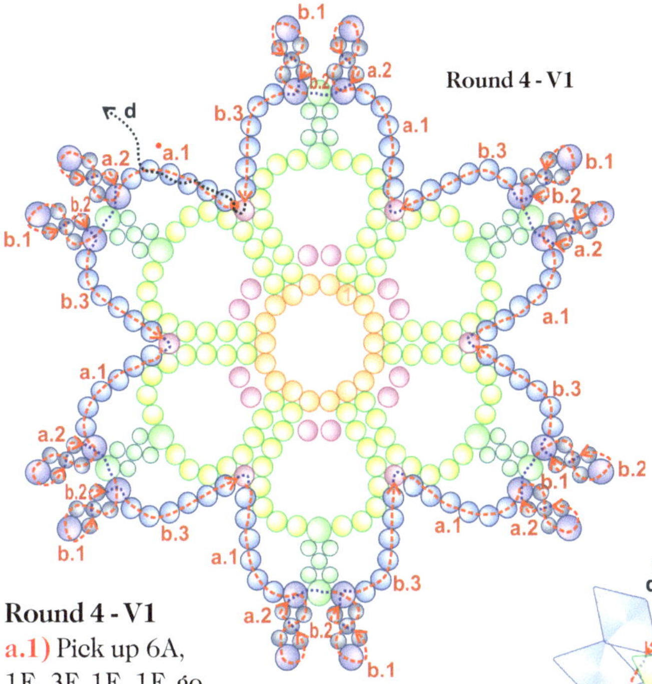

Round 4 - V1

Round 4 - V2

Round 4 - V1

a.1) Pick up 6A,
1E, 3F, 1E, 1F, go
with thread down
through the 2nd F bead just added.

a.2) Pick up 1F, go with thread right to left through
the 1st E bead added at (a.1) and the 2nd E bead,
R2V1a.1.

b.1) Pick up 1E, 3F, 1E, 1F, go with thread
down through the 2nd F bead just added.

b.2) Pick up 1F, go with thread right to left
through the 1 E bead added in this Round at b.1.

b.3) Pick up 6A, go with thread left to right
through the 1 A bead, R3a.

c) Repeat (a.1, a.2, b.1, b.2, b.3) around 5 more
times. .

d) Continue with thread up through the 1st
through 5th A beads added in the first repeat of (a)
in this round.

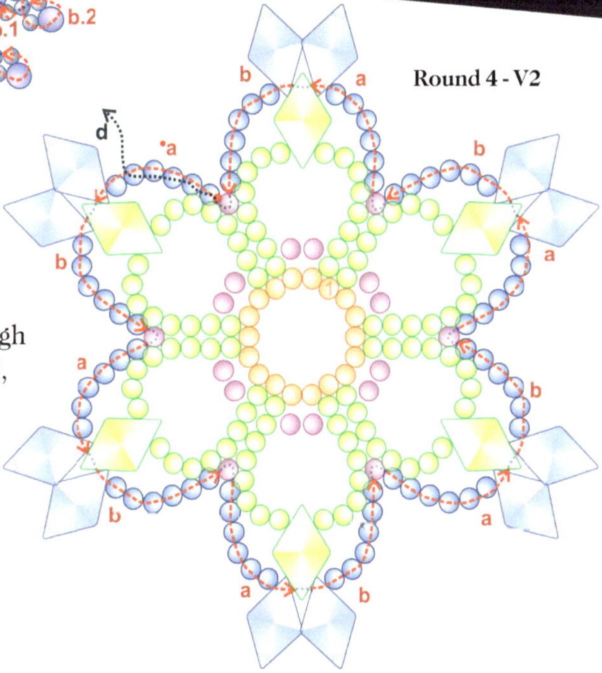

Round 4 - V2

a) Pick up 6A, 1D, go with thread right to left
through the top hole of the D bead, R2a.

b) Pick up 1D, 6A, go with thread left to right
through the 1 A bead, R3a.

c) Repeat (a, b) around 5 more times. .

d) Continue with thread up through the 1st
through 5th A beads added in the first repeat of (a)
in this round.

Round 5 - V1

a) Pick up 5A, go with thread right to left through the 2nd E bead, R4V1a.1.

b.1) Pick up 1A, 1B, 2A, 1B, 2A, go with thread forward through the 1st B bead just added

b.2) Pick up 1A, go with thread right to left through the 2nd E bead, R4V2b.1.

c) Pick up 5A, go with thread down through the 2nd through 4th A beads, R4V1b.3.

d) Pick up 1B, 2A, 1B, 2A, go with thread forward through the 1st B bead just added and up through the 3rd, 4th and 5th A beads, R4V1a.1.

e) Repeat (a, b, c, d) around 5 more times.

f) Continue with thread up through the 1st through 4th A beads added in the first repeat of (a) in this round.

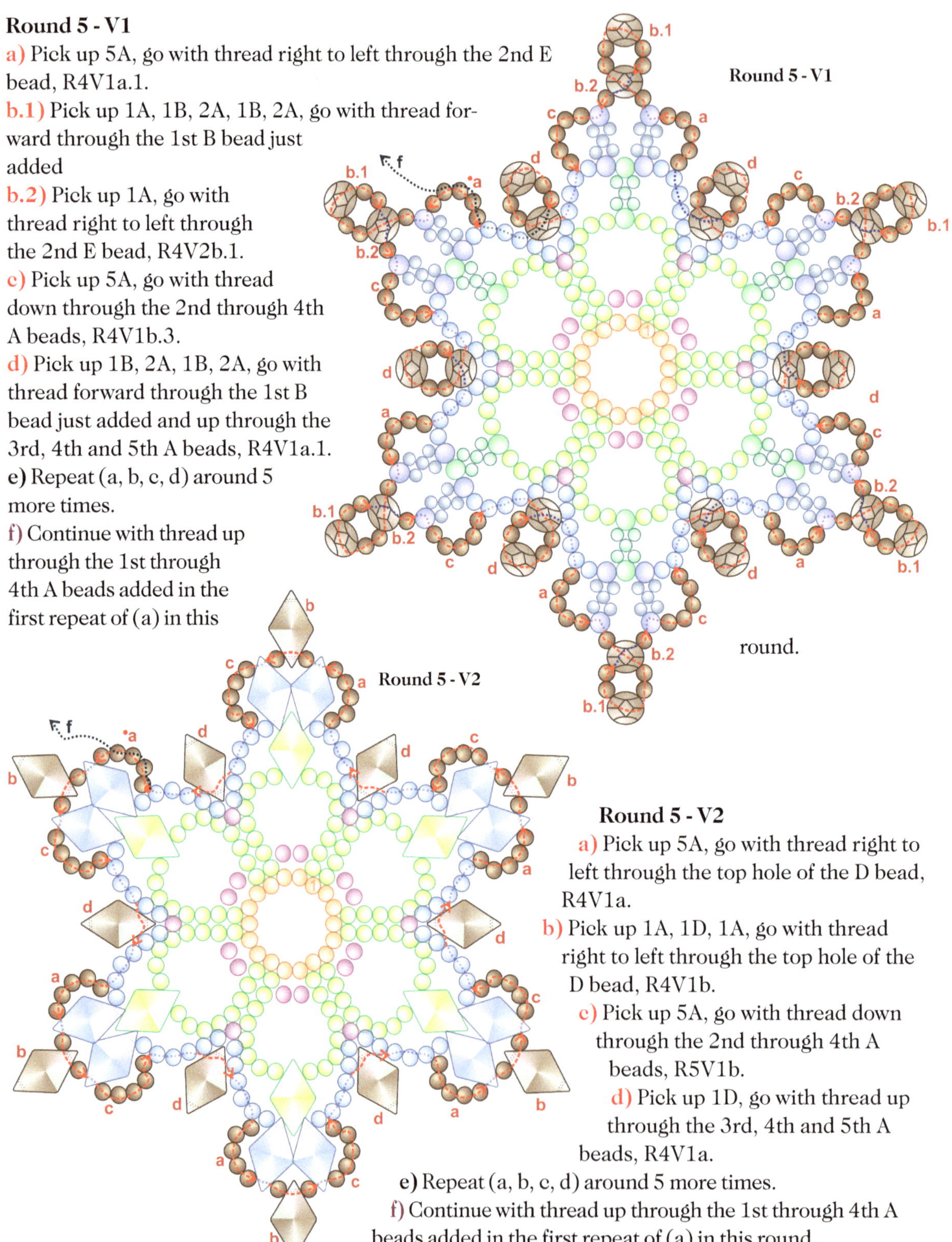

Round 5 - V2

a) Pick up 5A, go with thread right to left through the top hole of the D bead, R4V1a.

b) Pick up 1A, 1D, 1A, go with thread right to left through the top hole of the D bead, R4V1b.

c) Pick up 5A, go with thread down through the 2nd through 4th A beads, R5V1b.

d) Pick up 1D, go with thread up through the 3rd, 4th and 5th A beads, R4V1a.

e) Repeat (a, b, c, d) around 5 more times.

f) Continue with thread up through the 1st through 4th A beads added in the first repeat of (a) in this round.

Round 6 - V1 and V2

a) Pick up 3A, go with thread up through the 4th and 5th A beads, R5a.

b) Pick up 6A, go with thread forward through the 3rd A bead just added.

c) Pick up 2A, go with thread right to left through the 2nd B bead, R5V1b.1 or the top hole of the D bead, R5V2b.

d) Pick up 6A, go with thread forward through the 3rd A bead just added.

e) Pick up 2A, go with thread down through the 1st and 2nd A beads, R5c.

f) Pick up 3A, go with thread down through the 2nd and 3rd A beads, R5c.

g) Pick up 2A, go with thread right to left through the 2nd B bead, R5V1d or the top hole of the D bead, R5V2d.

h) Pick up 2A, go with up through the 3rd and 4th A beads, R5a.

i) Repeat (a, b, c, d, e, f, g, h) around 5 more times.

j) Continue with thread right to left through snowflake coming and going through the 1st, 2nd, 6th and 5th A beads added in the first repeat of (b).

Round 6 - V2

Round 7 - V1 and V2

a) Pick up 3A, go with thread up through the 5th and 4th A beads, R6b.

b) Pick up 7A, go with thread forward through the 4th A bead just added.

c) Pick up 3A, go with thread right to left through the 6th and 5th A beads, R6d.

d) Pick up 3A, go with thread right to left through the 5th A bead, R6d.

e) Pick up 4A, go with thread down through the 2nd A bead, R6f.

f) Pick up 3A, go with thread right to left through the 2nd A bead, R6g, the top hole of the D bead, R5V1d or the 2nd B bead, R5V2d and the 1st A bead, R6h.

g) Pick up 3A, go with thread up through the 2nd A bead, R6a.

h) Pick up 4A, go with up through the 5th A bead, R6b.

i) Repeat (a, b, c, d, e, f, g, h) around 5 more times.

j) Weave the working thread into the snowflake and end.

Glitz Snowflake Ornament
2-1/2 Inches

Version 1

A = Miyuki 11° SEED bead,
    420 beads

B = 3 mm Fire-polished crystals,
    12 crystals

C = 4 mm Fire-polished crystals,
    12 crystals

E = Miyuki 8° SEED bead,
    6 beads

Version 2

A = Miyuki 11° SEED bead,
    420 beads

C = 4 mm Fire-polished crystals,
    6 crystals

W = Twin Beads,
    18 beads

E = Miyuki 8° SEED bead,
    6 beads

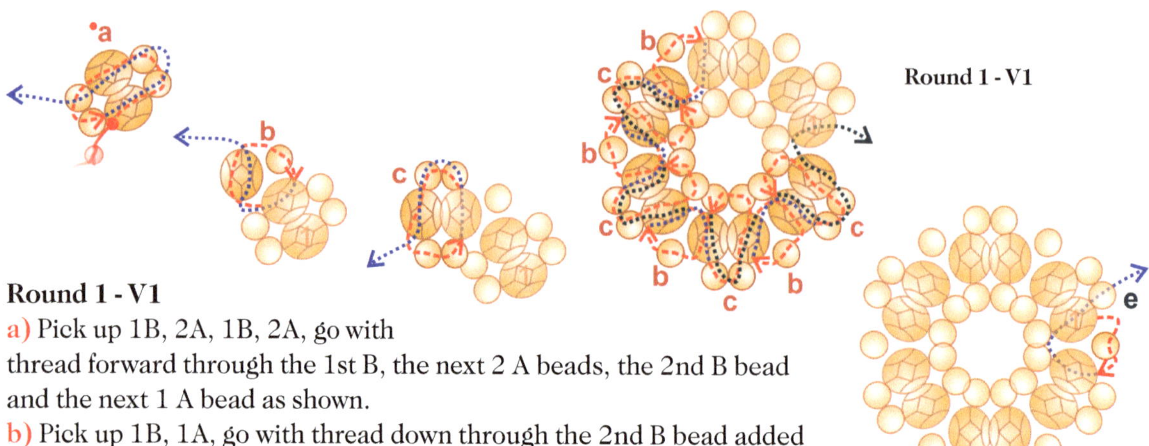

Round 1 - V1

a) Pick up 1B, 2A, 1B, 2A, go with
thread forward through the 1st B, the next 2 A beads, the 2nd B bead
and the next 1 A bead as shown.
b) Pick up 1B, 1A, go with thread down through the 2nd B bead added
at (a) , or the 1 A bead added at (c), and forward through the B bead just
added in this step.
c) Pick up 2A, 1B, 2A, go with thread up through the B bead added in the last step and forward
through the 2 A and 1 B beads just added in this step.
d) Repeat (b, c) around 4 more times. After completing the last repeat of (c) continue with working
thread up through the 1st B bead added at (a).
e) Pick up 1A, go with thread down through the B bead added at the last repeat of (c), up through
the 1st B bead and the 1st A bead added at (a).

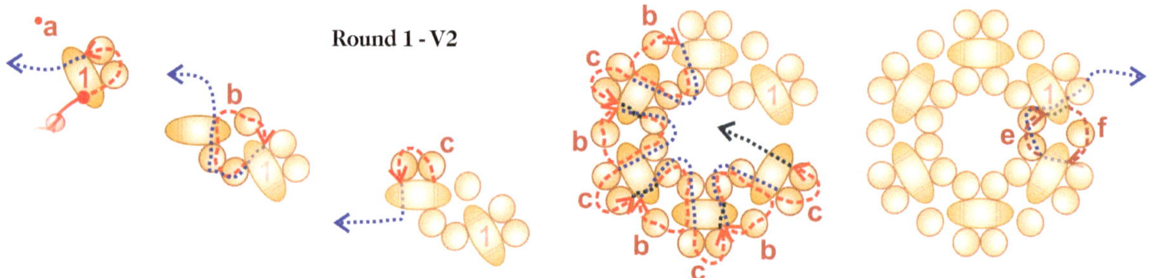

Round 1 - V2

a) Pick up 1W, 2A, go with thread down through the left side hole of the W bead just added.
b) Pick up 2A, 1W, 1A, go with thread down through the left side hole of the W bead added at (a) or
((b) in later steps) and forward through 2 A beads and the W bead just added in this step.
c) Pick up 2A, go with thread down through the left side hole of the W bead added at (b).
d) Repeat (b, c) around 4 more times.
e) Pick up 2A, go with thread up through the right side hole of the W bead at (a).
f) Pick up 1A, go with thread down through the left side hole of the W bead added at the last repeat
of (b), forward through the 2 A beads added at (e) and up through the right side hole of the W bead
and the 1st A bead added at (a).

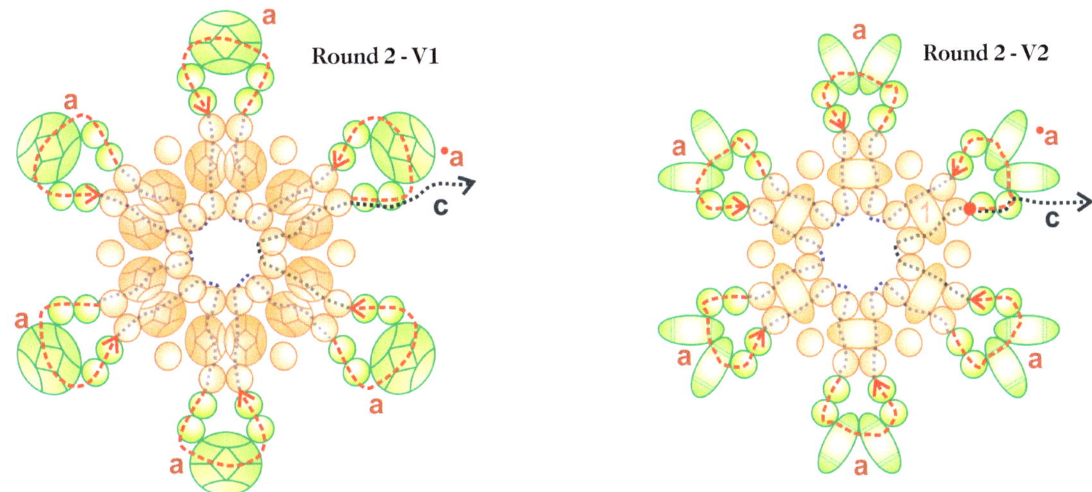

Round 2 - V1

a) Pick up 2A, 1C, 2A, go with thread down through the 2nd A bead, 2nd B and 3rd A beads, R1a, up through the 4th A bead, R1c, the B bead, R1b, and the 1st A bead, R1c, (First Time) or down through the 2nd A, the 1B, the 3rd A, R1c, up through the 4th A R1c, the 1B R1b and the 1st A, R1c, (every time after) as shown.

b) Repeat (a) around 5 more times.

c) Continue with thread up through the 1st and 2nd A beads added at the first repeat of (a).

Round 2 - V2

a) Pick up 2A, 2W, 2A, go with thread down through 2nd A bead, R1a or R1c, the W bead R1a or R1b, up through 2 A beads and the W bead, R1b and the 1st A bead, R1c, as shown.

b) Repeat (a) around 5 more times.

c) Continue with thread up through the 1st and 2nd A beads added at the first repeat of (a).

Round 3 - V1

This Round is worked Clockwise

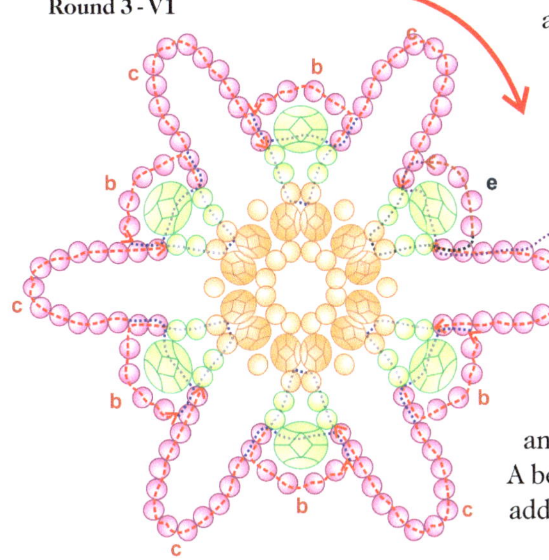

a) Pick up 15A, go with thread down through 3 A beads and up through 3 A beads as shown.

b) Pick up 6A, go with thread down through 14th and 15th A beads added at (a), or the 12th and 13th A beads added at (c), left to right through the C bead, R2a and up through 1st and 2nd A beads just added in this step.

c) Pick up 13A, go with thread down through 3 A beads and up through 3 A beads as shown.

d) Repeat (b, c) around 4 more times. Continue with working thread up through the 1st and 2nd A beads added at (a).

e) Pick up 4A, go with thread down through the 12th and 13th A beads added at the last repeat of (c), down 3 A beads and up 3 A beads and the 1st through 5th A beads added at (a).

Round 3 - V2
This Round is worked Clockwise
a) Pick up 15A, go with thread down through 3A beads and up through 3 A beads as shown.
b) Repeat (a) around 5 more times.
c) Continue with working thread forward through the 1st through 5th A beads added at the first repeat of (a) in this Round.

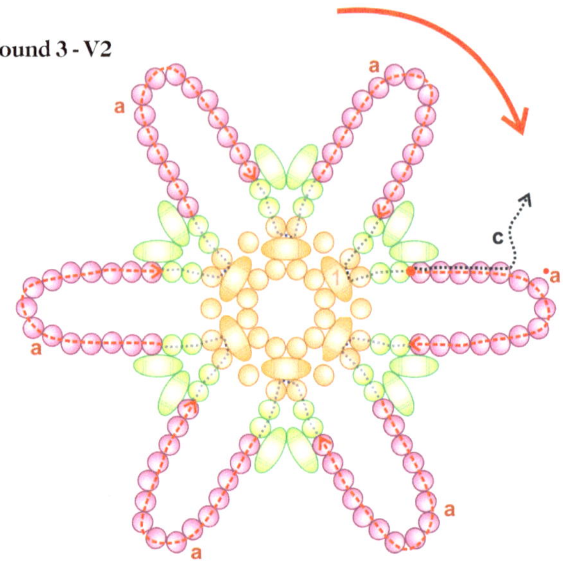

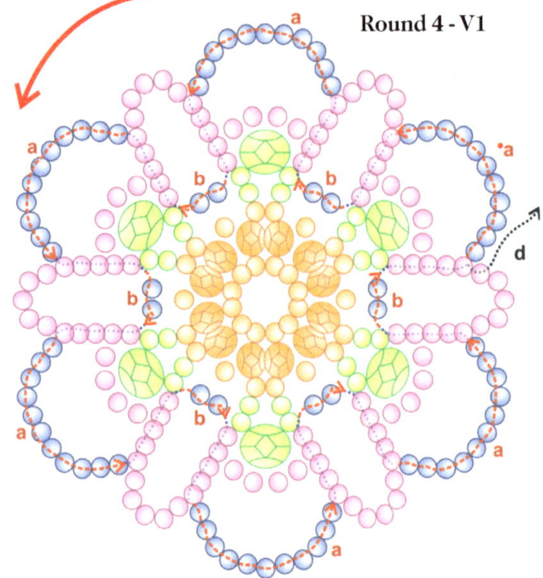

Round 4 - V2
This Round is worked Counter - Clockwise
a) Pick up 11A, go with thread down through the 9th through 13th A beads in R3V1c and the 2nd and 1st A beads, R3b (or at the last repeat go with thread down through 5 A beads in R3a as shown).
b) Pick up 2A, go with thread up through the 1st and 2nd A beads in R3V1b and the 1st, 2nd and 3rd A beads, R3V1c.
c) Repeat (a, b) around 5 more times.
d) Continue at the last repeat go with thread up through 1st through 6th A beads in R3a as shown

Round 4 - V2
This Round is worked Counter - Clockwise
a) Pick up 11A, go with thread down through the 5 A beads in R3a as shown.
b) Pick up 2A, go with thread up through the 5 A beads in R3a as shown.
c) Repeat (a, b) around 5 more times.
d) Continue with thread up through 1st through 6th A beads, R3a.

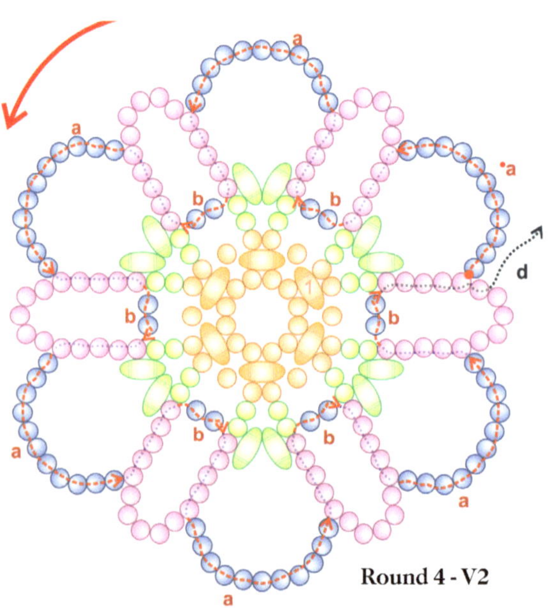

Round 5 - V1

a) Pick up 15A, go with thread down through the 8th, 9th, 10th and 11th A beads, R3V1c, (or on the last repeat go with thread down through the 10th, 11th, 12th and 13th A beads in R3a as shown.
b) Pick up 1C, go with thread up through the 1st, 2nd, 3rd, and 4th A beads, R3c.
c) Repeat (a, b*) around 5 more times.
d) *After the adding the C bead at the last repeat of (b) go with working thread down through the 2nd A bead, R3V1a and through the 1st and 2nd A beads R3V1e.

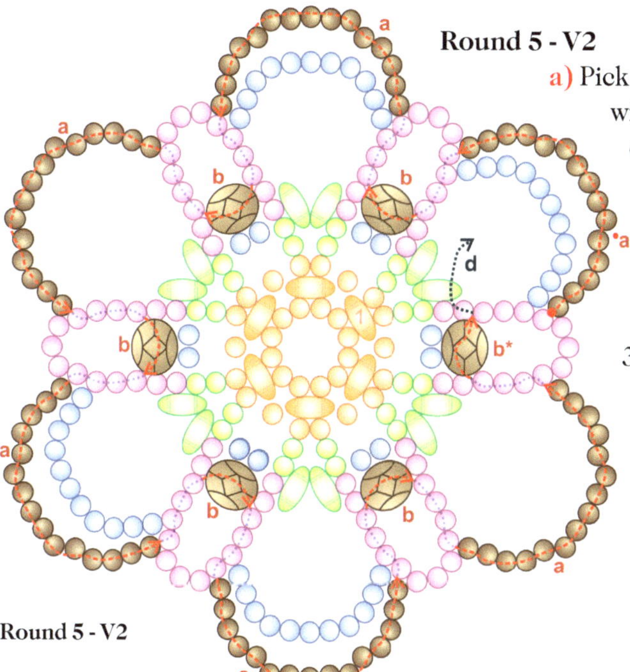

Round 5 - V2

a) Pick up 15A, go with thread down through the 10th, 11th, 12th and 13th A beads, R3V2a.
b) Pick up 1C, go with thread up through the 3rd, 4th, 5th and 6th A beads, R3a.
c) Repeat (a, b*) around 5 more times.
d) *After adding the C bead at the last repeat of (b) go with working thread down through the 2nd A bead, R3V1a and right to left through the top hole of the 1st W bead, R2V1a.

Round 6 - V1

a) Pick up 1E, go with thread right to left through the 3rd and 4th A beads, R3V1e, or right to left through the 5th and 6th A beads, R3V1b, down through the 12th A bead, R3V1c, right to left through the C bead, R5V1b, up through the 2nd and right to left through the 3rd and 4th A beads, R3V1b.
b) Repeat (a) around 5 more times.
c) After repeating the last repeat of (a), continue with working thread up through the 2nd, 3rd, 4th, 5th and 6th A beads, R3V1a and the 1st, 2nd, 3rd and 4th A beads, R5V1a.

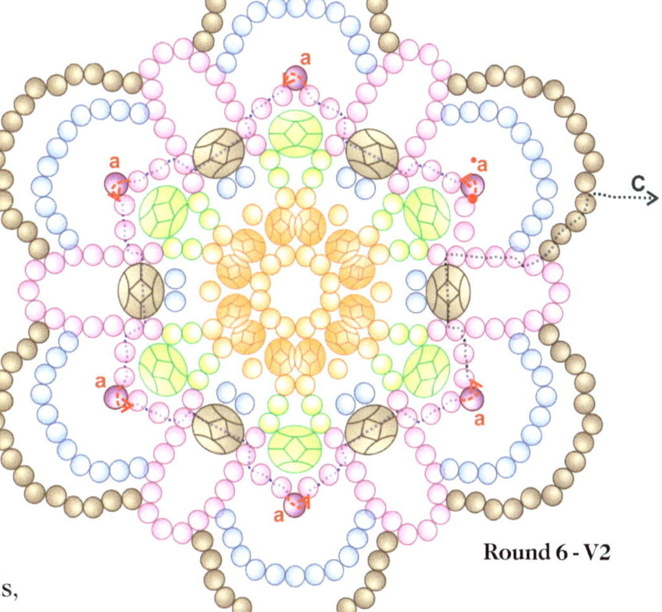

Round 6 - V2

a) Pick up 1E, go with thread right to left through the 2nd W bead, R2V2a, up through the 14th A bead, R3V2a, right to left through the C bead, R5V2b, down through the 2nd A bead, R3V2a and right to left through the 1st W bead, R2V2a.

b) Repeat (a) around 5 more times.

c) After repeating the last repeat of (a), continue with working thread up through the 3rd, 4th, 5th and 6th A beads, R3V2a and the 1st, 2nd, 3rd and 4th A beads, R5V2a.

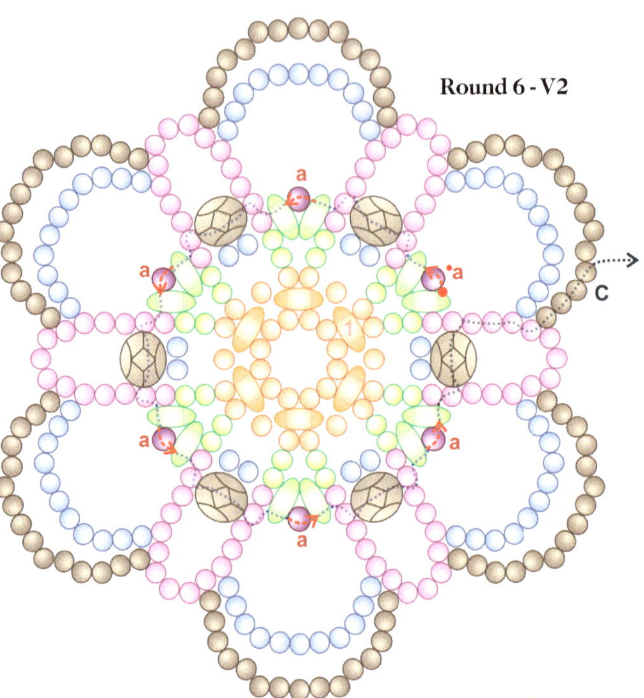

Round 6 - V2

Round 7 - V1 and V2
This Round is worked Counter - Clockwise

a) Pick up 3A, go with thread forward through the 4th, 5th, 6th and 7th A beads, R5V1a or R5V2a.

b) Pick up 5A, go with thread forward through the 2nd A bead just added in this step.

c) Pick up 1A, go with thread forward through the 9th, 10th, 11th and 12th A beads, R5V1a or R5V2a.

d) Pick up 3A, go with thread forward through the 12th, 13th, 14th and 15th A beads, R5V1a or R5V2a, down 4 A beads, R3, right to left through the C bead, R5 and up through 4 A beads, R3, right to left through the 1st through 4th A beads R5V1a or R5V2a, as shown.

e) Repeat (a, b, c, d) around 5 more times.

f) Weave the working thread into the snowflake and end.

Round 7 - V1 and V2

Snowflake Finishing

Making Hangers for your Snowflake

or a piece of pretty ribbon.
Add ribbon after your snowflake is stiffened.

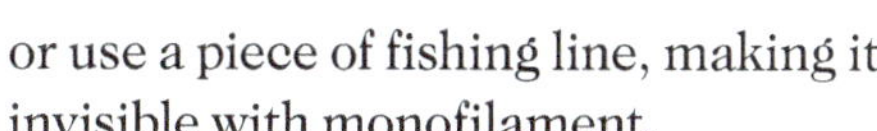

or use a piece of fishing line, making it
invisible with monofilament,

Make it with beads, make a loop with as
many beads as you would like,

Finishing

After the snowflake is complete, you can stiffen it with SC Johnson Pledge Future Shine. It is a great stiffener, it stays clear even on the crystals. Test it first if you use seed beads with dyed colors to make sure the floor finish doesn't remove the colors.

Pour enough of the Future Shine into a small container that is wide enough for the ornament. Float the ornament into the Future® Shine and push it around a bit with your finger. (After I am done, I use a funnel and pour the extra back into the bottle)

Take the ornament out and blot both sides with a paper towel.

Put the ornament on a piece of wax paper, shape and flatten it and let it remain on the wax paper to dry. (If you use plastic wrap, the beads can stick a bit to the wrap, so it needs to be moved around a bit to prevent this from happening.) If your ornament needs a little extra flattening, use two pieces of wax paper and sandwich your ornament in between; put a book on top of the wax paper for about an hour. Take the book and the top piece of wax paper off the ornament and let dry overnight on the bottom piece of wax paper.

Optional Stiffener for your snowflakes

1 TBSP Corn Starch
1 Cup cold water
1 TBSP White Glue

Wax Paper or plastic Wrap
Paper Towel
Old Pan
Tablespoon
Whisk
Something to swish your beadwork
around (I used a plastic fork)

This mix is a great optional stiffener for your snow-flakes, especially if the Floor shine is not available.

Test first if you use seed beads with dyed or lined colors to make sure this mix to make sure it doesn't remove the colors.

Start by whisking together 1 Tablespoon of corn starch with 1 cup of cold water in your pan. Heat just to boiling while whisking in 1 TBSP of white glue. Continue whisking until the mixture starts to boil. Take off of the burner and let cool.

Float your snowflake ornament in the mixture and push it around a bit with your plastic spoon (mine is a fork). Leave for a couple of minutes and then stir around one more time before taking it out to dry.

Take the ornament out and blot both sides with a paper towel. Be especially mindful of your crystals that you rub the mixture off.

Put the ornament on a piece of wax paper, shape and flatten it and let it remain on the wax paper to dry. (If you use plastic wrap, the beads can stick a bit to the wrap, so it needs to be moved around a bit to prevent this from happening.) If your ornament needs a little extra flattening, use two pieces of wax paper and sandwich your ornament in between; put a book on top of the wax paper for about an hour. Take the book and the top piece of wax paper off the ornament and let dry overnight on the bottom piece of wax paper.

Thats it!
Clean up is easy too and no lasting odor.
Enjoy your new snowflakes.

Blot both sides of your snowflake with a paper towel